A God Thing
The Small-World Phenomena
Spiritual Frequency

John S. Lee

A God Thing: The Small-World Phenomena Spiritual Frequency

The events and conversations in this book have been set down to the best of the author's ability, although some names and details have been changed to protect the privacy of individuals.

© Copyright 2022 John S. Lee

All rights reserved. No part of this publication may be reproduced or transmitted in any form or by any means without written permission from the publisher.

Unless otherwise indicated, all Scripture quotations are taken from the *Holy Bible, New International Version* (NIV). Copyright 1973, 1978, 1984 Biblica. Used by permission of Zondervan. All rights reserved.

Scripture quotations marked NASB are taken from the *New American Standard Bible*, Copyright 1960, 1971, 1977, 1995 by The Lockman Foundation. Used by permission. All rights reserved.

Scripture quotations marked NKJV are taken from the *New King James Version*. Copyright 1982 by Thomas Nelson, Inc. Used by permission. All rights reserved.

Cover and interior design by Marji Laine
Edited by Lori Freeland

ISBN: 979-8-9861616-1-7

Published by:

 Roaring Lambs Publishing
17110 Dallas Parkway, Suite 260
Dallas, TX 75248

Contact the author at:
revelation_409@yahoo.com
FB Page: @agodthingbook

Published in the United States of America.
Printed in the United States of America

Dedication

To Jesus Christ
for giving His approval and support
for me to write this book.
It wouldn't have been possible
without Him
because there would be no story
without Him.

Table of Contents

Dedication 5
Foreword 7
Acknowledgments...9
Introduction 11

PART I
Small-World Phenomena..13

Chapter 1: Seek and You Will Find 15
Chapter 2: Small-World Phenomena 25
Chapter 3: The Road to Jesus....................................35
Chapter 4: Waking up to God's Presence 61
Chapter 5: Healing 77

PART II
The 409 Revelation...87

Chapter 6: Origins of the 409 Revelation..................89
Chapter 7: Anniversaries and Dates 97
Chapter 8: Celestial Symmetry 113
Chapter 9: Formula 409 Cleaner............................. 117
Chapter 10: People and Things.............................. 125
Chapter 11: Sandy the Dolphin and Scuba Diving .. 135
Chapter 12: Why Me? 141

A Final Word... 147
Sources 149
Notes 150

Foreword

*Many are the plans in a person's heart,
but it is the Lord's purpose that prevails.*
Proverbs 19:21

As someone who enjoys planning ahead, I often find myself struggling to trust God in times of stress or despair. It takes a strong relationship with Him to be able to give up control and have complete faith in His plan. John S. Lee, who I have the pleasure of referring to as Dad, has discovered how to discern God's purpose for his life by following signs that fall in line with his own spiritual frequency—the way he "tunes" into God's voice. My dad's trust in his spiritual journey has truly captured how someone can develop and grow their personal relationship with God by being open to His messages.

I'm honored to have been present through the early workings and experiences that have influenced the making of this book. Throughout my adult life, my dad has shown me how different situations and people are uniquely connected through "small-world phenomena." As a result, I've learned to look for the "coincidental" events—that aren't always so coincidental—and the intricate ways in which we're all connected.

My dad has an affinity for science and numbers. When he became a born-again Christian as an adult, it was a great accomplishment for him to learn to receive messages from God that appealed to his scientific nature. These messages served as guideposts to let him know he was going in the right direction. The messages became the journal entries that ultimately led to the creation of this book, and I'm so thankful to finally see it come to fruition.

My dad's connection to God, first through "small-world phenomena" and later through the more specific "409 revelations," has not only strengthened his faith over the years but has been an inspiration to those around him. Witnessing his experiences has influenced me to be more mindful of my own personal faith journey, especially in the ways God chooses to connect with me.

As a counselor, I believe it's vitally important to live a life that helps others and serves God's greater purpose. The human psyche is delicate and should be nurtured in a way that meets each person's unique needs. One of the best ways to nurture the soul is to seek support and guidance through your own spiritual journey. I look up to my dad for his courage and passion to share his story. The next time you discover a unique connection in your own life, I encourage you to think of it not as a coincidence but as *A God Thing*.

Alyssa Jones, LPC, CRC
Licensed Professional Counselor
Certified Rehabilitation Counselor

Acknowledgments

Ghie, my wife, thank you for being supportive and understanding throughout this long process.

My late mother, Gayle, who was always supportive of my projects and theories.

My late father, Ed, for not insisting on his career choices for me, which allowed God and I to determine my path.

Alyssa, I appreciate you. Thank you for writing the foreword, for your advice, and for agreeing to take over the authorship of this book in case something happened to me before it was finished.

Lana, my sister, your advice and content was so important to this book.

To Juliana, my baby granddaughter, thanks for giving me additional hope for the future. Watching you grow up will be a real joy and motivation to stay alive.

Also to my dog, Angel. You were the best therapy dog during my cancer treatments and a great lap dog while writing this book.

Texas Oncology at Texas Health Resources (THR) Dallas, thank you for keeping me alive and keeping my spirits up while undergoing chemo for leukemia as I wrote this book. Dr. Barve and Taylor— the nurse assigned to me—did a great job as did the rest of the staff.

A God Thing

My publisher, Roaring Lamb Ministries, including Marji Laine and Donna Skell who both helped and influenced this book. Thank you for putting it together.

Lori Freeland, my editor and writing coach, your hard work and expertise greatly enhanced the book.

And a huge thank you to all the pastors who shared their theology with me, including Keith Stewart, Kevin Ritzi, and the late Irvin Baxter.

I know I've missed others, so if you participated in this book in actions or ideas, thank you too!

Introduction

"In this life we all experience moments, sometimes so unique or unusual that we pause and say, Wow…what are the odds that could happen? And if something like that happens again, maybe we say it's just coincidence. How many once-in-a-lifetime events do we attribute to simple chance before we believe that perhaps it's something more? At what point do you ask yourself, is it just luck or have I experienced a miracle?"
~ Mike Lindell
What Are The Odds?
From Crack Addict To CEO

Mike opens his bestselling book with the words above. Although our stories differ, they also have similarities—including close brushes with death, unlikely occurrences, encounters with people that we didn't expect, and miracles that were most likely of divine origin. His book resonated with me and has inspired me to share my stories.

PART I
Small-World Phenomena

A God Thing

Chapter 1
Seek and You Will Find

So I say to you, ask, and it will be given to you;
seek, and you will find; knock, and it will be open to you.
For everyone who asks receives, and he who seeks finds,
and to him who knocks, it will be opened.
Luke 11:9–10 NKJV

Before December 2004, I was an agnostic. While I believed in the possibility that God existed, I didn't care that much and definitely wasn't ready to "come to the Lord." Then one day, I discovered Christian talk radio. More accurately, God led me there. But I couldn't see that then. Through listening to the programs, I began to seek Jesus and develop a relationship with Him. As time went on, He drew me to church and Bible studies. The more I sought, the more I found.

That's what I'm hoping will happen for you and may be a reason this book is in your hands. God draws us to Him in different ways, meeting His people at every level of their personal faith journeys. The wonderful thing about

A God Thing

His approach is that He uses our interests to get our attention and speak to us. His revelations, so to speak, are rooted in what we care about and what we understand.

Since I found Jesus, I've grown so much in my knowledge and faith, yet I know I still have further to go in my Christian walk. I'm grateful that God consistently shares new revelations with me that guide me closer and closer to Him.

Writing a book was never my intention. It's hard work. Especially when you start out typing twenty words a minute. But the more I procrastinated, the more signs God sent to gently push me toward that keyboard.

The seeds for this book were planted in 2009 as I drove past campaign signs encouraging me to vote for Todd Meier—who ended up serving three consecutive terms as mayor of Addison, TX. Recognizing him from when we both attended Greenhill School, I emailed him. We met for coffee at a local Starbucks to catch up, reminisce about the class of '69, and share encounters we'd both had with former classmates over the years.

One of those classmates was a guy named Tom, who I'd gone to elementary school with. Years ago, I dreamed that he'd given his testimony. In it, he'd shared that he used to follow Satan—completely out of character for him—but had turned to Jesus. A decision that had changed his life. My clock radio went off, waking me to a *Focus on the*

Family broadcast of someone giving that same testimony.

Two weeks later, I happened to be listening to *America's Family Coaches* on the radio, and Dr. Gary and Barb Rosberg had a guest speaker from *Focus on the Family* . . . named Tom! He even shared the same last name as my Tom. It wasn't the same guy of course. This Tom lived in Des Moines, Iowa. But he had lived in Richardson, Texas, back in 1986. Interesting. I got married in 1986, and I lived in Richardson and was president of the Dallas Divers Club in Richardson in 1986.

After I told Todd about the dream, we talked about another classmate, Craig. I'd attended F.P. Caillet Elementary School with both Tom and Craig. Todd said, "I went there, too. What are the odds?" The odds were pretty remarkable considering there were just forty-six people in the class of '69, only half of them boys, and students came from all over the Dallas area to go to our private school.

On a sidenote, Todd asked that question years before Mike Lindell made a similar statement. If you missed it, you can find Mike's quote at the beginning of this book. What makes this even more interesting is that Todd had been the mayor of Addison—the same city where Mike was honored by Roaring Lamb Ministries in 2021.

When I mentioned writing a book, Todd encouraged me. Up until then, I hadn't been all that serious. Maybe I was supposed to reach out to him so he could light a fire

A God Thing

under me to do God's will.

A month later, I was trying to listen to talk radio while I waited in the car for my coworker Mary. Working in home health care, I often drove the nurses to see patients and helped with the care if they needed me to lend a hand. Radio reception was always staticky in Sherman, Texas. I'd pretty much given up on 91.7 FM when Point of View suddenly came through loud and clear just as Kerby Anderson was interviewing Karol Ladd and Donna Skell of Roaring Lamb Ministries about their upcoming 2009 Christian Writers Conference. The event, held in Addison in July, would connect new and potential authors with more established authors and provide information on how to put ideas into book form and how to publish.

Two weeks later, Carol, a business associate, called and asked me to video a project for her—a side gig I did part-time. I agreed, but let her know I couldn't do it the next weekend because of the conference. She told me she might like to go with me. Interestingly, our call took place in front of the patient's home where I'd first heard about the event.

That same day, I listened to Andrew Wommack on *The Gospel Truth*. I got out of his message that we needed to do something with our spiritual authority to get things accomplished for God, and that even if what we did was not perfect, God could and would use it. Wow. That really spoke to me.

Between the conference being in Addison, where Todd had given me the initial encouragement, the radio station reception clearing up in time for me to hear about it, the phone call with Carol, and Andrew Wommack's words, I couldn't ignore God's prodding. So, I went to the conference and prayed on the way, "Lord, I know that You want me to go, but I'm still not sure if You actually want me to write a book. Please give me signs." And He did.

Gene Getz of *Renewal Radio* and an author of over forty books opened the event. He passed out the first two chapters and some of the third chapter of Nehemiah from his Bible commentary *Principles to Live By*. He also shared his humble beginnings in publishing and how he hadn't been good at composition or very confident about writing at first. I could relate, and his story gave me hope.

After that, we split into three different writing tracks. I chose nonfiction by Jody Capehart and Karol Ladd. Karol had been a math and science teacher before she became an author and hadn't seen herself as a writer. When I told her that sounded a lot like me, we had an instant connection.

One of the ladies at my table lived in Richardson like me. One of the men lived in Carrollton—a place I rarely went. Yet I'd gone there the night before on business. Another man was a pastor at a Baptist church near Webb Chapel and LBJ, where I'd lived for many years.

A God Thing

After lunch, Kerby Anderson—the host of *Point of View* where I'd heard of the conference—led another general session. He gave away his book *Making the Most of Your Money in Tough Times* to whoever had the birthday closest to his. That was me. We shared the same December 7 birthday.

Sandra Glahn spoke next and talked about an accident she'd had on—of all dates— December 7—that had powerfully influenced her writing.

Jan Winebrenner closed out the conference, posing the question, "Is God calling you to write?" She referred to a quote from Frederick Buechner. "Your deep gladness must match the world's deep need." Encouraging us to transform our operating system to the ways of God, she said we shouldn't necessarily make it our goal to become a writer if it wasn't God's will. It wasn't about us. It was about Him and His Glory. By this time, I was pretty sure God was waving His arms trying to get my attention.

The morning after the conference confirmed it. My daughter Alyssa and I went to Springcreek Church in Garland where Pastor Keith Stewart preached on a series called "Deliver Us from Me-Ville." The message lined up with Jane Winebrenner's as Keith said, "Put God first, not self." He also used the book of Nehemiah in his sermon and referenced the same chapters included in Gene Getz's sample handouts.

Keith said, "If you had a vision from God, it's going to take more time than you have, it's going to take more people than just you, and more resources than you've ever seen. When you know that, you'll look at that situation and say, 'My God what have I got myself into? I can't possibly do this.' And this is where visions stall. People hear from God, they see this amazing thing that God wants to do, it's so much bigger than they are, and then they say, 'Well I can't do this.' That's where we're wrong in our thinking. Nehemiah makes clear that God asks us to step out in faith before we know all the facts, where all the resources are coming from, and who all the people are that are going to help us. Where God's agenda is championed, God's resources are channeled."

Sometimes we feel called to a task we're confident we can accomplish. When that happens, there's a chance it isn't from God but from our own desire. While He does use accomplished people—like Luke, the physician and Greek scholar, who wrote one of the Gospels—more often than not, He uses unaccomplished people.

Other times we feel called to a task we're not confident we can accomplish. When that happens, God probably did call you to it. The good news is that He will also help you through it. Look what He did through Moses and Gideon, both people with weaknesses. Moses spoke with a stutter, yet he became a great leader of the Jews and marched them out of Egypt. Gideon considered himself the least of the least—the least tribe in Israel, the least family in his tribe, and the least within his family—but his leadership turned out to be very effective against the Midianites.

Between that sermon, the signs pushing me to attend the conference, and everything I experienced while I was there, there was no doubt God wanted me to write this book. That didn't change the fact that I still only typed twenty words a minute and the task felt incredibly daunting. So, I prayed for his help. An hour later, I discovered an email about Dragon Naturally Speaking 10, a device that turns speech into typed words. The first answer to my prayer? I ordered it and used it for the first draft of this chapter. That was many years ago. Now that my typing has improved, I don't need it as much, but it got me started when writing felt impossible.

Recently, I found out I have leukemia. I've had cancer before and wasn't blissfully ignorant of the journey to come. Chemo, blood transfusions, and other unpleasant procedures loomed on the horizon. Very disappointing, as I'd hoped to be done with cancer for the rest of my life. I didn't blame God, but I dreaded living through those treatments again.

Once I regained my composure over the news of my diagnosis, I came to the conclusion that the leukemia was meant to be. For one, it put me in a humbler state of mind to obey God's calling to write this book. And two, it sped up my timeline. He'd given me a strong message months ago that I'd interpreted as, "Yes, John, I still want you to write the book. What are you waiting for?" And that message suddenly made so much more sense.

Over the years, God has helped me accomplish the tasks He's called me to. He quickly answered my prayer about this book to reassure me I was on the right path and He was walking beside me. He's drawn me to Him and shown me who He is and what He wants to do in my life. And I know He'll do the same for you. All you have to do is ask and be ready to see what He wants to show you and listen to what He wants to tell you.

A God Thing

Chapter 2

Small-World Phenomena

*I have seen something else under the sun:
The race is not to the swift or the battle to the strong,
nor does food come to the wise or wealth to the brilliant or favor to the learned; but time and chance happen to them all.*
Ecclesiastes 9:11

The most popular definition of small-world phenomena is the idea of "six degrees of separation" in a social sense. John Guare wrote a play with that title in 1990. Also referred to as the human web, it's the idea that any one person is—at most—six people away from knowing any other person. This dates back to Karinthy Frigyes's short story written in 1929 about people who played a game to see how they were connected to others all over the world. Michael Gurevich, Stanley Milgram, and other academics have also conducted research studies on the topic.

My personal awareness of small-world phenomena began with the popular TV series *Lost*. It was both sci-fi and spiritual—two things of great interest to me. The

A God Thing

premise involved a plane crash, a hidden island, and survivors who should've been killed on impact but weren't. Episode by episode, we learn nearly all the characters have met each other or met a person acquainted with someone on the plane *before the accident.* The purpose of these connections becomes apparent in the finale. It turns out that a spiritual force arranged for that group of people to bond with each other in a sort of purgatory to prepare them to go to Heaven together. Even though God was never brought up, it's my interpretation that He was the spiritual force that shaped the experiences of the characters just as He's the spiritual force that shapes my destiny and yours.

When I first talked about small-world phenomena, I referred to it as the *Lost* phenomena, but I quickly realized not everyone was as passionate about the show as I was. Now, I refer to it as the small-world phenomena, which others do as well. Except my definition goes beyond the social network to include other factors such as dates, numbers, places, unexpected encounters, and against-the-odds phenomena. Sort of like the signs that pushed me to write this book.

Over the years, I've learned to pay attention to these things as well as to dreams and visions. Remember that God finds us where we are and speaks in ways that are meaningful to us. He tries to get my attention and tell me about Himself through small-world phenomena. Hence, my initial love for *Lost*.

Some people see repeating patterns and human connections as coincidences. Sometimes they are. But when a roadmap can clearly be seen, I'm convinced things don't happen by chance but by divine providence. There are theologians who take this position too. I heard an excellent message once about divine providence by Richard Ellis from Reunion Church. What I got out of it was there's a time and purpose for everything and a plan and direction for everyone's life. Like tuning to a certain station to find Christian talk radio, I tune into a spiritual frequency to find God and receive His revelations for my life.

One Sunday, I watched an episode of *The Big Bang Theory* where Sheldon, one of the main characters, mentioned *Lost*. Thirty minutes later, my family and I attended service at Springcreek Church. That morning, Pastor Stewart's sermon "The Gift of Friendship" directly related to *Lost's* big reveal that people were destined to meet. He said, "Friends are not made, they are given." To paraphrase a quote by C S Lewis, "God prepares a banquet of people He wants to connect."

There are other fictional and true stories that support this idea. Mike Huckabee shared one on FOX News about an eleven-year-old, homeless, black kid named Maurice. Living with parents stuck in a drug culture they felt they couldn't escape, Maurice approached a white lady named

A God Thing

Laura Schoff and asked for money because he was hungry. While most people's instinct is to ignore panhandlers, that wasn't what happened with Laura. Maurice's hunger resonated with her so deeply that she invited him to have lunch with her at McDonald's. That one lunch turned into weekly lunches, and their relationship completely turned his life around. He left the drug culture, became the owner of a small construction company, and went on to marry and have seven kids. Eventually Maurice and Laura set up a charity to help the homeless. Their friendship is still going strong decades later.

This story opened my eyes and gave me a more compassionate understanding of the homeless. With a little help, they didn't necessarily have to stay in dead-end situations. Laura wrote a book about what happened with Maurice called *An Invisible Thread* that gives insight into the interconnectivity of people who are destined to meet.

That reminded me of the TV series *Touch*. Like *Lost*, it takes patterns and numbers a little further when it comes to forming a roadmap to connect people who need to find each other. The main character Jake—an eleven-year-old autistic savant—is the one who discovers all the interrelationships in the show. It stuck out to me that Jake happened to be the same age as Maurice.

A less spiritual show called *Num3ers* ran for six years at the same time as *Lost* and was about solving federal crimes using mathematics. I noticed several things that tied into some of my small-world phenomenon occurrences, and the finale dealt with six degrees of separation.

Then there was *Manifest*—another show I identified with that had sci-fi and spiritual elements. The first episode opens with the mysterious return of flight 828—presumed lost for the last five years. The returned passengers, all thought to be dead, soon realized they might be meant to do things far beyond anything they ever could've imagined. Some of the events and important numbers interconnected with my world and pointed me to Romans 8:28, a verse appropriate to my life during that time. "And we know in all things God works for the good of those who love him, who have been called according to his purpose."

This idea that certain people and groups who ride the same currents of life are intertwined for a common destiny can be described in a secular way too. A great example comes from Season 1 in award-winning Episode 28 of the '60s nostalgic sci-fi series *Star Trek*. In *City on the Edge of Forever*, the USS Enterprise encounters ripples in time produced by a machine on a distant planet. After Dr. McCoy accidentally injects himself with a substance that makes him crazy, jumps through the time portal, and changes history, Kirk and Spock go back in time to try to set things right.

Soon after they arrive on Earth in 1930, Spock tells

A God Thing

Kirk, "There is a theory. There could be some logic to the belief that time is fluid, like a river, currents, eddies, backwash."

To which Captain Kirk replies, "And the same currents that swept McCoy to a certain time and place might sweep us there too."

Spock agrees.

Although fictional, I like to think that suggests how God operates. Perhaps He designed the universe in such a way that people and events in a certain place and time are destined to flow together.

The TV series *Criminal Minds* brought to my attention the idea of synchronicity. In Season 11, Episode 2, "The Witness," FBI profiler Dr. Tara Lewis discovers she's connected to a serial killer she's hunting when she learns their mothers attended the same elementary school. Agent David Rossi quotes Paul Author, saying, "We are ruled by the forms of chance and coincidence." Later, FBI team member Dr. Spencer Reid is shown reading the book *Synchronicity: An Acausal Connecting Principal*, and he states that synchronicity is "events that seem significantly related but have no acausal connection." Then he tells Lewis, "Maybe the events in our lives were set in motion a long time ago," and refers to a Buddhist saying that the "act to bring together soulmates is five hundred years in the making."

Swiss psychiatrist, psychoanalyst, and founder of analytical psychology Carl Jung believed that meaningful coincidences play an important role in people's lives. This idea appears in many beliefs around the world. My oncologist, Dr. Barve, even mentioned something similar in India. Some people look to synchronicity for spiritual guidance. In Christianity, this is divine providence.

I remember Pastor D. G. Hargrove of North Cities United Pentecostal Church mentioning something about how when a pastor preaches a sermon, God has a way of speaking to each person individually, tailoring His message to where they are in life and what they need to hear. That's why the Bible is called the Living Word. It means something new in different times of our lives. I believe God can align the universe so that each of us can receive a message that means something unique and special while not altering any other person's reality or destiny.

We all have a destiny. God has a purpose for everyone. For those who seek Him, He will reveal what He wants us to do through the things that most interest us. This is how each follower of Jesus will learn to find their own spiritual frequency.

Small-world phenomena seems to work well for me. It may also work for you. From the moment I first realized that God used small-world occurrences to get my attention, I began to focus on them. In other words, I tuned into that spiritual frequency to see what God was trying to show me, which led to revelations. As I've grown in the Word, I've improved my ability to discern the meaning of what God shows me, and it's easier to figure out what He wants me to do. Whether this is something you're interested in or not, I encourage you to get to know God better by seeking His Word and learning to tune into the way He chooses to communicate with you.

Jeff Wickwire of Turning Point Church hosted a radio program called *Life Talk*. One day when I was listening, I recall him describing the remarkable way God operates. Using biblical examples, he talked about how God revealed things to people in the way they understood. For instance, God used an angel to communicate the future birth of Jesus to the Virgin Mary. He also used angels to inform the shepherds that Jesus had just been born. As Jews, angels are what they understood and would be looking for. However, the three wise men from the East who desired to give gifts to the infant Jesus were astronomers, so God created a special star for them to follow. These examples helped me understand why God used my interest in science fiction in the visions He gave me while I was in the hospital fighting cancer back in 2002. I describe this more fully later in the book. But even if you never receive signs and visions, you can get plenty of revelations and instructions from reading God's Word.

This is a good place to talk about being cautious when it comes to signs and visions. Please understand that they don't replace or change what God has already revealed. In fact, signs and visions are dangerous without a firm foundation in the Bible. That's why it's important to be familiar with the Word. If a sign or vision contradicts what you know of God, be suspicious. Do your research to see if it aligns with scripture.

Did you know that Satan and his demons can also perform what appear to be miracles, signs, and wonders? The Bible warns us to avoid all forms of the occult and worshipping Satan. "There shall not be found among you . . . one who uses divination, one who practices witchcraft, or one who omens, or a sorcerer, or one who casts a spell, or a medium, or a spiritist, or one who calls up the dead" (Deuteronomy 18:10–11 NASB).

At the end of the age, which some believe may be fast approaching, the false prophet will perform great signs and deceive many. Revelation 13:13–14 states, "He performs great signs, so that he even makes fire come down from heaven on the earth in the sight of men. And he deceives those who dwell on the earth to make an image of the beast that was wounded by the sword and lived" (NKJV). But if you have the discernment to know what is and isn't from God, signs can reinforce the Bible.

God wants you to seek Him. He wants to connect with

A God Thing

you wherever you are in your spiritual journey. He wants to speak to you through your interests. Throughout this book, my goal is to show you how I developed a personal connection with Jesus Christ in the hope that you might develop your own.

Chapter 3

The Road to Jesus

> *"No temptation has overtaken you except what is common to mankind. And God is faithful; He will not let you be tempted beyond what you can bear. But when you are tempted, He will also provide a way out so you can endure it."*
> 1 Corinthians 10:13

As I look back on my life before I knew Jesus, I see ways in which He was working in me even then. Before I really understood anything spiritual, I had unusual experiences that were spiritual in nature. Even as a child, God allowed me to witness strange and fascinating events. In 2008, I decided to journal my small-world phenomena going back as far as the '60s. Here are a few descriptions of them that helped lay the foundation for me to later develop a greater relationship with Jesus.

FIN AND FEATHER

Back in 1962 when I attended F.P. Caillet Elementary

School in northwest Dallas, my family had a membership to Fin and Feather. This club on a lake in Hutchins had seven hundred acres and offered hunting and fishing. Limited to just forty-one families, it was about twenty-five miles from my house.

One weekend, I recognized a girl at the boathouse from my fifth-grade class. Surprised to see Helen, because of the small number of members and the distance from school, I definitely mentioned it to her on Monday. This was my earliest memory of a small-world phenomenon occurrence.

Dreams

In the summer of 1968, right before my senior year of high school, I had a dream about this short guy I worked with in the cafeteria of the Presbyterian Hospital of Dallas. In real life, we didn't like each other. That carried over into the dream.

In the dream, he'd parked his '56 Chevy in my neighbor's driveway. Now Debbie, the definition of the "girl next door," I liked a lot. She and her father were talking on her back porch while the guy waited for her, and I stood off to the side. From what I heard, it seemed like the guy and I were in competition for her. As the discussion wound down, he walked toward his car. As he passed me, we looked at each other, turned away, then did a double take. That's when I woke up.

Later that day, I went to work at the cafeteria. As I dumped trash into a small room near the exit, the short guy came down the hall toward me, and we ended up eyeing each other just like in the dream—right down to the double take. The setting might've been different, but everything else was the same. An episode of the original TV show *The Twilight Zone* outlined similarities between dreams and reality and helped me see the connection between the two.

I had another dream in the '90s I won't ever forget. In it, Satan offered me worldly possessions and great status—if he got my soul when I died. I politely told him that while his offer was tempting, the price was too great and declined.

Some theologians believe God plans our lives and determines our destinies. I don't disagree. This very unusual dream seems like a perfect example of Him moving in my life, getting me ready to meet Him. Even more so considering at that point I hadn't given religion or Jesus much thought. That would come later, and that's when the dream took on more meaning.

UFO ENCOUNTERS

Some of the first unusual events I journaled were my

A God Thing

UFO encounters. In the past, there had been a stigma about UFO sightings. For the longest time, I didn't believe mine and certainly didn't reveal them to anyone other than close friends. Today, the military and mainstream media are both reporting these sightings, including Tucker Carlson on FOX News. So, I'm going to share what I saw with you.

February 1968
Farmers Branch, Texas

One day in the spring of my junior year of high school, I was walking alone with my pellet gun near a creek in a semi-wooded area of the Dallas suburbs. The neighborhood off the intersection of Marsh Lane and Valley View Lane had been an abandoned private property estate back then and a good place to look for plinking targets and do some shooting.

A hundred feet ahead of me, a silver-metallic, football-like object lay on the ground. Despite being a big science fiction fan and a die-hard follower of the original *Star Trek* TV series, the thought that it might be a UFO didn't occur to me. My first instinct was to shoot at it. The pellet "pinged" off the object. Just as quickly, the object shot up at a 45-degree angle—with what seemed to be light speed—and instantly vanished.

That's when I began to think about the possibility that "football" might've been some sort of small UFO craft.

For the record, I was not under the influence of drugs or alcohol or prone to hallucinating. Nor had I ever been.

Although I wanted to tell the whole world, I ended up telling only a select few people. Because most of them agreed I'd probably been hallucinating, I doubted what I saw and decided to keep quiet about it. Until now.

December 2010
Garland, Texas

Over forty years later in the church parking lot after a Bible study, I stayed after to talk with some friends. One of them had an infrared video camera pointed toward the night sky and stumbled onto something he thought was strange. Handing me the camera, he told me to look.

Through the viewfinder, I saw a small dot of whitish light moving rapidly. Suddenly, without slowing down, it made a right angle turn and kept going. The camera was passed around to the others, and they witnessed the event as well.

Afterward, I shared my first UFO sighting with the group. One of the women disagreed with the hallucination theory I'd been holding onto and told me she thought what I'd seen had been real. Between her belief in me and the TV series *Hangar 1: The UFO Files* on the History Channel, I finally found legitimacy for what I'd experienced.

A God Thing

While most of the first season didn't relate to my experiences, there were a few episodes in the second season that did. Episode 5, "Star People," shared the story of a UFO on the Navajo Reservation in Arizona shot with a high-powered rifle in June 2010. The craft immediately sped to the left just like my high school encounter. Episode 7, "UFO's Over Texas," mentioned an egg-shaped UFO the width of a highway seen by several people in Levelland, Texas, in November 1957. That was the first time I'd heard of another UFO besides mine with that shape. Episode 12, "UFO Superpowers," reported someone had seen a basketball-size UFO in a house in Miami in March 2012.

Those events felt like a sign for me to go ahead and report my first experience. In July of 2015, I finally decided to tell the Mutual UFO Network (MUFON) what I'd witnessed. A nonprofit organization consisting of civilian volunteers, MUFON studies UFO sightings. I thought maybe sharing my experience could provide a bigger picture within their case file or offer information that would resurface in future sightings or reports. If you're interested in reading it, it became MUFON case file #67799.

These UFO sightings are just one example of the out-of-the-ordinary experiences in my life that eventually led me to God.

John S. Lee

NEAR FATAL DRIVING ACCIDENTS

In the '70s, I went hunting at the Belknap Ranch out in Frisco on New Year's Day. If you were familiar with this suburb of Dallas back then, you might remember it as being very small. The downtown consisted of one tiny country store and gas station. Nothing like what you'd find there now as one of the fastest growing and largest cities in the Dallas/Fort Worth (DFW) area.

Heading home on Highway 289, I approached the Highway 121 intersection going around 70 mph. The roads were iced over, and for some reason, I didn't have my seatbelt fastened like I normally would.

Out of nowhere, a car pulled out in front of me.

My first instinct was to brake. Not the best idea. My car swerved, sending me toward oncoming traffic. Quickly changing tactics, I let off the brake. Right before I was about to slam into the back of the car that had cut me off, I was somehow able to steer to the right shoulder of the road. After doing an abrupt one-eighty, I ended up in a ditch. While other drivers slowed down to rubberneck, I checked out the car—and myself. There was not one scratch on either. I got back on the highway and drove home as if nothing had happened.

If I would've hit that car—which I almost did—between my speed and the icy road, the collision would've

A God Thing

certainly killed me and whoever else was involved. Although I didn't yet know Jesus, I knew enough to recognize that as a miracle.

A few years later, I dodged another bullet after a scuba diving trip to Possum Kingdom Lake. Driving home with Scott—who'd been my friend since elementary school—and my boat hitched to my car, I saw a sign off the highway that said Mineral Wells was twenty miles away.

Tired, I wanted to ask Scott to take over, but he'd already fallen asleep. I decided to tough it out. The next thing I remember is coming out of a daze to a sign stating that Mineral Wells was ten miles away. What had happened to those other ten miles while I was unconscious? I could've easily run off the road or hit another car—which could've been deadly. God gave me another miracle.

Jump forward to the summer of 1990 when I learned to drive an eighteen-wheeler. I'd just completed my controlled-track training. It was my first day on public roads with the instructor and other students. I wasn't that sure of myself considering I'd be maneuvering that huge truck in traffic.

Although it was a hot day with no icy roads, the exact same thing that had happened in Frisco roughly twenty years prior happened again. A car pulled out in front of me. I wasn't sure how, but I made all the right moves to avoid an accident. I even remembered to pull on my horn. The instructor was furious at that other driver. I was just happy to have my third miracle and to survive once again.

I took all these "near miss" accidents as signs that it was not my destiny for major harm to come to me at those times. And that furthered the idea that God had plans for me in the future.

The Unexpected

Have you ever unexpectedly done well in a situation where you thought for sure you'd fail? Or unexpectedly failed in a situation where you thought for sure you'd do well? I have. Sometimes there's no explanation as to why, but after everything I've learned about faith, I'm thinking it's a God thing. When I look back at these kinds of events, I wonder if there was a spiritual element involved that pulled me out of my norm so I could see the positive and negative spiritual influences in my life at different times.

Although I wouldn't say I ever expected to fail at ping-pong, I have a great example where I went above and beyond my natural abilities. Scott, from the Possum Kingdom story, remained one of my best friends during my college days. When we both came home on breaks, we liked to play competitive ping-pong. At first, I played better. But over the years, he steadily improved, becoming a worthy opponent who gave me real competition. One evening, we

A God Thing

were playing in my garage, and I was close to losing my lead.

Then something suddenly changed. In *Star Wars* terms, the force was with me. Scott couldn't touch me. In fact, he was only able to score a couple of points. In his words, I was "playing way over my head." I have no idea what happened. But the timing of it was interesting. That match—where out of nowhere, I temporarily gained the abilities of a world champion—occurred just as ping-pong championship games were beginning to open the door to United States and China relations.

Another time in the '70s, I got together with a few friends for a game of wits. We all wrote something down on a piece of paper and tried to guess each other's item. Bill, the intelligent guy in the group, kept winning all the rounds. Frustrated, I was determined to come up with a strategy to beat him. Then an idea popped into my head. I wrote down his name, and it stumped him. When I won, he complimented me.

On the other hand, I went into my freshman year math class at Southern Methodist University (SMU) with full confidence, positive I would succeed. Even though I didn't take calculus in high school, I wasn't worried. I'd been a straight A math and science student. I'd get an A, no problem. To my total shock, I got a D both semesters. I wanted to blame it on the way it was taught—rapidly and in large chucks. Because of that, there was a chance I'd missed an important step and got lost as new material had been introduced. Understandable.

Except . . . the last six weeks of second semester covered analytic geometry. A subject I knew well and had studied in high school, where I'd been at the head of my class with a 98 average. Again, I was confident going into that final six weeks of calculus knowing I'd surprise the professor with my tremendous turnaround performance. Even better, no new material was added, and the topic didn't even go into as much detail as it had in high school. I took the final exam for that section and waited to get the news that I'd aced it. I actually made another D! How could that happen? Devastated, I thought about going to the instructor and challenging a possible mistake in the grading. Instead, I took that D as a sign to change my major.

The same thing happened on a Dallas Divers Club trip to Rum Cay in the Bahamas. With a talent for underwater photography and a history of winning or placing in photography contests, I took what I thought were going to be amazing pictures. After the slides were developed, I was disappointed to discover them to be very mediocre. You can see why I wasn't eager to share them with the club, but I reluctantly did.

A God Thing

Post College

One of my first jobs after college graduation was at a small supply company in Dallas that employed around six people. My department only had three guys—one of them shared my name, John. Single at the time, I decided to try a dating service. To my surprise, the girl I matched with turned out to be that John's girlfriend's daughter. The small size of the company against the backdrop of the large city made this extra amazing.

Several months later, I attended a Dale Carnegie night course. One of the twenty or so other students was Robert H. Dedman Jr., son of philanthropist Robert H. Dedman. My parents were members of his country club, Brookhaven. Robert Jr. was a senior at Greenhill, where I'd graduated five years before. He also went on to become a philanthropist. One of the many boards he served on happened to be Southern Methodist University (SMU), where I'd graduated the year before.

Lyda Hill, daughter of Margaret Hunt Hill and granddaughter of H. L. Hunt of the famous Hunt family, also attended that Dale Carnegie class. My dad ran into H. L. Hunt a couple of times. First when he sold some packaging machinery to one of Hunt's businesses. Second at an airport waiting for a flight to Dallas, where they talked for three hours. Note that there were multiple generations involved and that these connections came up again in later events.

The generational connections with the Hunt family get more interesting. I mentioned that Roaring Lamb Ministries honored Mike Lindell. The other honoree was June Hunt, H.L. Hunt's daughter. I told my sister Lana, and she said she knew June. They'd been sorority sisters in college back in the '60s and had played bridge together. Lana knew about the conversation between H.L. Hunt and my father and shared more on the encounter. Lana also stated that while she was in high school, Mr. Hunt had found out she wanted to be a nurse and had given her some great advice about nursing school. He'd suggested she study Latin to make it easier. She did, and he'd been right.

I also discovered my own ties to June. In addition to the Roaring Lambs Christian Writers Conference in 2009, I also attended in 2010, where June Hunt was the lunch keynote speaker. Like Karol Ladd the year before, June mentioned that English and literature weren't her favorite subjects and that she had a stronger interest in math and science because they were more logical. This was a huge reinforcement of how my small-world phenomenon experiences became more interconnected over time.

A God Thing

ROARING LAMBS CONFERENCE 2022

During my third Roaring Lamb Ministries Christian Writers Conference in June 2022, the small-world occurrences kept coming. It seemed like the closer I got to the release of this book, the more I saw them all around me. About to turn in the final draft of the manuscript, I was looking for some professional advice on publishing and marketing. I took my daughter, Alyssa, with me. There were many great speakers, and we both learned a lot.

When we arrived, Alyssa recognized one of the ladies helping out at the desk through a work connection and ended up telling her a little about my book. After we checked in, we found a table, and I sat next to a guy named Morris—who the lady ended up knowing through a charity organization. That "coincidence" piqued her interest, and she took it as a sign to keep on the lookout for my story. How amazing that it was already having an impact even before its release.

Also at our table was someone I wasn't expecting to see—an acquaintance from the Filipino American community I've known for a long time. Next to her sat a young woman who was involved with communications studies at SMU, my alma mater. Interestingly, the ladies knew each other through charity organizations. And I discovered my fellow SMU alum had been a judge for the Miss Asian

American Texas Pageant, where I used to be the official videographer. It's likely we were both there at the same time.

The talk of pageants led to a conversation on the upcoming Miss Texas America Pageant taking place that night. One of the candidates, Averie Bishop, had ties to the Filipino community in North Texas. But the small-world phenomenon gets even better. Back in 2009, Alyssa won the Miss Philippines Texas Pageant, and Averie won the Miss Teen Philippines Texas, which ran simultaneously. Averie went on to win many other pageants as well as the Miss Texas crown later that night. History was made as she was the first Asian American to win.

CORE LABS

In 1975, I joined Core Laboratories, a much larger company than I'd previously worked for. I spent about four years in the mailroom and then moved onto the lab. One day, President and Chairman of the Board John Wisenbaker toured the building. When he met me, he offered his hand. Immediately, I pulled back my gloved hand and told him it was covered in mercury and oil. One of the things I appreciated about him was that he made a point to shake my dirty hand anyway. And it seemed important to him that he did. Starting from those early days in the mailroom,

A God Thing

he took an interest in me, partly because I offered him some advice on scuba diving and underwater photography.

I soon discovered Core Labs used Hill World Travel, owned by Lyda Hill, and it was my understanding that the Wisenbaker family was connected to the Hunt family. Over the years, my association with John Wisenbaker flourished at Core Labs. And he let me know I was always welcome at his front door.

An interesting thing happened after that. In 1986, I'd just begun dating my future wife, Ghie, who'd been staying with her friend Luz. As a nanny, Luz lived over the garage of the family who employed her. When I went to visit Ghie, I noticed a piece of paper on Luz's table with John Wisenbaker's daughter's name on it. Luz confirmed he was her employer. After I told her about my relationship with him, she gave me a tour of the house. I stood underneath his portrait chuckling over the fact that while I'd been welcomed at his front door anytime, I'd come through his back door instead. And he never knew.

On a different note, had Luz not offered Ghie a temporary place to stay, our relationship would've never gotten off the ground. In our circle of American and Filipino friends, tension between me and a few of my acquaintances made it awkward for Ghie and I to date. And at thirty-five, opportunities to find the right lady continued to slip through my fingers. I don't know how my life would've turned out without Ghie. I might've ended up marrying someone who wasn't good for me. Although no marriage is perfect, my wife is amazing. She has stuck by me even when I didn't deserve her devotion. Had our destiny to be together been divinely determined? That was a strong possibility.

Back to Core Labs and my first job in the mailroom. In those early days, the responsibility for handling the mail for the large multinational company fell on just me. One day, I picked up a letter in the tax department from Mary, the secretary. She'd addressed it to Becky Graves in Nacogdoches, Texas. One of my best friends from elementary school through college had been Gordon Graves who'd also graduated from Steven F. Austin State University in Nacogdoches. Curious, I asked about the letter. Mary said Becky was her sister and at the time was married to Gordon. I believe this small-world phenomenon occurrence was more than just a coincidence.

Within a year, Core Labs had grown so much they added another person to the mailroom under me—my first supervisory assignment. I don't think the woman liked me very much as she often refused to acknowledge what I asked her to do. Some of the department secretaries made complaints about her too. While I struggled to work with her, I tried to represent her fairly. When she performed well, I let my supervisor know. However, when she was let

A God Thing

go several months later, I wasn't heartbroken.

A week or so later, I got a call from the lady who ran the bank next to Core Labs, where we routinely did business. She asked about my former employee's performance. Realizing if I didn't tell the truth that it would reflect badly on me if she got hired and it didn't go well, I was honest. And she didn't get the job.

Not long after, she turned up in the teller window of my personal bank down the street from my house. In an awkward moment, she sheepishly said hello to me. When I got home, I called the manager and expressed my concern that she might be holding a grudge against me. That made me nervous considering she had access to my money. The manager had concerns as well but couldn't do much about it except keep a close eye on her. The uneasy feeling that I carried around about her had me constantly looking over my shoulder and lasted longer than she did at that job. Sometimes I wonder where she ended up.

In contrast to that experience, I had a great coworker later in another department. As a close friend of the Wisenbaker family, Cynthia had been referred by John directly. She and I got to talking one day, and I discovered she was Carey's sister, a girl who'd been in my Greenhill class of '69.

During my time in the mailroom, we eventually grew

to four people. I was in the Office Services Group that included the three guys in maintenance. Rich, the youngest member, was also a part-time chaplain with other organizations. Because the mailroom was right next to maintenance, we worked in close proximity, and I got to know him pretty well.

Eventually, I got a promotion and transferred to the Reservoir Fluids Lab (RFL), where I performed analysis on oil and gas samples. A few months later, I got a call that something happened to my father and I needed to hurry to Parkland Hospital in Dallas. When I arrived, my mother and some other family members told me my father had committed suicide. The chaplain assigned to my family was Rich. He also performed the graveside ceremony. Grateful for his presence, I was glad for the opportunity to have gotten to know him as a coworker before I knew him as a chaplain.

When I went back to work, things were strange. My coworkers knew something, but I wasn't sure what. I never talked about what happened. Years later, Larry—one of the friends at work that I'd met before all that happened—mentioned that my dad's death must've been one of the best-kept secrets at Core Lab because he'd never heard about it. Rich had never said a word. I appreciated him even more after that.

A God Thing

POST CORE LABS

The petroleum industry was in decline in the late '80s. I left Core Labs to work in a more healthy industry—environmental labs—from the early to mid-'90s. My duties included analysis of liquid and soil samples to determine the content and quantity of pollutants. I first worked for NDRC Laboratories, which eventually became Inchcape. Later I worked at Certes. My manager, Joe, had gotten hired there first and then hired me. An interesting sidenote is that in all the departments and companies I worked at, Joe was my boss and manager.

He was also my neighbor and lived a couple streets over until several years later when he bought and moved to twelve acres of land in Princeton, Texas. I tried to call Joe in 2019 but didn't have his current phone number. I ended up sending him a letter with my contact information. He said that just before receiving my letter, he'd been thinking about hiring me to do VHS to DVD transfers for him. In his own words, he called that a "small-world phenomenon situation." Wow! We eventually got together at his place and caught up.

Shortly afterward, I had a conversation with my next-door neighbor David, and he mentioned he was from Pittsburg, a small town in East Texas. Joe, who I'd just been thinking about the day before, was from there too. Back in the '90s, David, Joe, and I were all living in the same neighborhood. David mentioned that his family owned the only dry cleaning store in Pittsburg, and Joe confirmed that. It was another small-world phenomenon occurrence involving Joe. That made two in a row.

Post Environmental Labs

In the late '80s, while I still worked at Core Labs, my wife and I were invited to dinner at our friend's home in Allen. Rico worked at Atlantic Richfield Corporation (ARCO) at a petroleum research facility in Plano. Rico and his wife, Purita, had also invited his current lab assistant Joe—not my boss Joe—who'd also been at Core Labs in the past.

In the mid to late '90s, Rico offered me a job as a research technician in his Rock Mechanics Lab. I also helped out in other labs and rounded out my petroleum work experience to include different departments from those at Core Labs. I was very grateful that Rico gave me this opportunity to expand my knowledge in the petroleum industry.

Joe, Rico's former lab assistant, was still at ARCO in an adjacent department. We got to know each other a lot more. One day, he told me he was from Nacogdoches, Texas, where I had previously gone to Stephen F. Austin

State University (SFA) for a semester back in the early '70s. Then something occurred to me. His last name was the same as the student apartments I'd stayed in as a guest a few times. Joe confirmed his family owned them. Look at that. Another small-world phenomenon situation that popped up every decade.

CANCER: ROUND 1

Because I believe God wants to connect with all of us in an individual way, I also believe He uses whatever it takes to get our attention. It didn't matter that Jesus wasn't really on my radar yet. I was on His. Sometimes we have to be broken to be receptive and open to meeting Him in a personal way. Cancer did that for me. It was a call to action—to hear, listen to, and seek God's voice.

In the spring of 2002, I felt ill. Weak with a loss of appetite, I just figured I was a little bit under the weather. Luckily, Ghie is smarter than I am and insisted I see a doctor. I went expecting to be sent home to rest. Instead, I found out I had advanced-stage, large cell Non-Hodgkin's lymphoma.

The medical plan was to treat my fourteen centimeter tumor with chemotherapy one week at a time in the inpatient unit at Presbyterian Hospital of Dallas. There was a 25% chance I wouldn't survive. Although that meant I had a 75% survival rate, I wasn't comfortable with those odds. Feeling numb and unsure about something totally out of my control, I didn't dwell too much on it. And I certainly didn't see it as a spiritual shake-up at the time.

While in the hospital, I had an unusual experience. To pass the time during chemo, I sometimes watched TV. One day, the news came on and reported the gruesome story of Andrea Yates who killed her kids because the devil told her to. As I listened to the story, a deep sadness came over me, and I sobbed over man's inhumanity to man. News events don't usually affect me like that. I'm not an emotional person. But that day, it was as if I felt the way Jesus would've felt about such a terrible tragedy. Perhaps the Holy Spirit used this to pay me a visit and soften my heart for what was to come.

That May, I was scheduled for an angiogram to fix the veins in my chest that had been squeezed by the tumor. Sedated, I waited in the hall outside the operating room. While there, I saw a red, mesh net with squared off corners that completely covered my bed with me underneath it. At the time, I didn't know what to think, but I wasn't alarmed. Just curious.

A few months later, I had a conversation with Deborah, a home health nurse who also worked in an intensive care unit (ICU) in Mesquite, Texas. She told me that other patients had experienced similar visions of nets or shields.

A God Thing

Could my "hallucination" have been some sort of sign of divine protection?

After surgery, I recovered in the ICU where my wife worked. At the foot of my bed, I saw what appeared to be an almost square six-by-six-foot white cloud with a three-to-four-foot hole in the middle. Again, I was more curious than afraid. That cloud seemed to resemble a portal to another reality or dimension. Could it have led to another world or maybe even Heaven?

Why did I have that particular vision? Probably because I love science fiction. It makes sense that God would take that route with me. Even though I was on pain medication, it's still amazing how that type of vision fit into my imagination and suggested there may be more to life than a physical existence on Earth. I kept that in mind as I sought the Lord.

In 2009, I told my eighty-five-year-old mother about what I saw while in the hospital. Shocking me, she replied that for the first time in her life, she recently started seeing visions in the morning as she woke up. The first vision—of her falling out of bed—was more common. Later, she saw things like flowers. Scared at first, she got used to it but wondered if it meant her time might be coming to an end. She lived six more years. Unlike me, who had an idea why I saw what I did, it's hard to know exactly why she had those visions. When I get to Heaven, I'll have to ask her.

CANCER: ROUND 2

In 2021, cancer paid me another visit while I was writing this book. The second journey was very different from the first. Back then, I didn't know Jesus. And He wanted to get my attention so I would notice Him. Now I do know Jesus. And He wants me to tell my story so other people will notice Him too.

Many of the stories in this chapter are interconnected. Coincidence? I don't think so. Through the patterns bringing them together, I see something more. I see God leading me to an awareness of the small-world phenomena spiritual frequency. I didn't journal back in those days yet somehow remembered the details of what happened. I think God wanted me to share my life and point out how everything is linked.

Do you have stories that are linked? Try journaling things that happen to you. You might be surprised to find patterns and interconnections. Is there anything you think God might want you to share with other people? Sharing your stories can help you and the people you're connected with grow spiritually just as it's helped me.

A God Thing

Chapter 4
Waking up to God's Presence

*For those who find me find life
and receive favor from the Lord.*
Proverbs 8:35

Irvin Baxter of EndTime Ministries was the first person to open my eyes to the truth of the Bible by pointing out some interesting prophecies during his radio show. One day at the end of 2004, long before I'd ever listened to Christian talk radio, I was driving one of our nurses to see patients, and she asked me to find a program called *Politics and Religion* on KVTT 91.7 FM. Reluctantly, I agreed. The show quickly caught my interest, and I started tuning in daily. Eventually, I helped Pastor Baxter's prophetic ministry with video shoots of their lesson programs. On Father's Day 2008, he baptized me. Although I'd been baptized as a baby, as an adult, it was important to me to declare my desire to be a follower of Jesus Christ.

In the early days of my Christian walk, *Politics and*

A God Thing

Religion led me to other programs that gave me a hunger for God, a will to witness, and the desire to pray. Around that time, KVTT 91.7 FM encouraged listeners to share how Christian talk radio had changed their lives. I wrote my testimony, which was read several times over the air. That boosted my faith and presented me with a new Christian perspective that highlighted each of my small-world phenomenon experiences with newfound clarity.

RIGHT TIME, RIGHT PLACE

Have you ever "accidentally" been at the right place at exactly the right time? I have. In 2008, my daughter, Alyssa, participated in a summer research project studying freshwater fish ecology that was sponsored by David Gillette, PhD in the Biology department at Austin College. It involved seining various creeks and tributaries off Lake Texoma and the Red River. I was asked to help on one of the trips but had no idea where we were going. As we approached Pottsboro, Texas, I entered familiar territory.

Dr. Gillette said we needed permission to be on the land. Little Mineral Creek just happened to be located on a former patient's property, and I turned out to be the perfect contact to make the introduction. While we explored and seined the creek, I found what resembled a Moses stick. I took it as a sign that my part in that adventure had been divinely designed.

ECHOES

When God wants to emphasize certain messages, I believe He creates an echo effect. Here's what I mean. Have you ever thought, spoke, or prayed about something only to have it reinforced later?

One of the first times I noticed this was at a stoplight by a freeway near my house. The car in front of me had a bumper sticker that read, "It's all about God." At that moment, Kay Arthur was on KVTT radio speaking those same words.

The echo doesn't always come right away. Do you remember the vision I had in the hospital of the cloudy square with a hole in the middle of it to the right of the foot of my bed? Years later, I found this verse about Zechariah. "Then an angel of the Lord appeared to him standing at the right side of the altar of incense" (Luke 1:11). Reading it gave me a better understanding of what I'd seen. I think God knew that discovering Zechariah's vision and noticing it was in the same position as mine would fortify my faith.

During work one day, I shared that story with Marlene, another nurse, as I drove her to a patient's house. A few minutes after our conversation, *Faith, Hope and Love* with Pastor Bob Nichols of Calvary Cathedral came on, and he shared the same verse about Zechariah.

I wondered if those types of experiences happened to anyone else. I discovered they did. Years later, Marlene told me about hers. On the way to church, she'd prayed about how most of us, her included, tended to set our earthly needs first and put Jesus on the back burner. The sermon that day was on that very topic.

She and I also talked about the difference between astrology—which, like witchcraft, goes against God's Word—and astronomy, which gives us legitimate signs like the star of Bethlehem. We listened to *The Prophecy Club* hosted by Stan Johnson on 1630 AM together, and the guest spoke on that subject. A double echo from God, emphasizing we should pay close attention.

Chance or Divine Providence

As I was paging through my journals, I found a story that reminded me of something Dr. R. C. Sproul, a prominent theologian from Ligonier Ministries, had shared on the radio show *Renewing Your Mind*. When I went to look for it, I ended up opening to that page in my journal.

Dr. Sproul gave a talk on knowing God's will. He asked, "Do things happen by chance or by divine providence?" He stated that the most traditional way to determine God's will was to seek His Word. But he also mentioned more unconventional means. He cited an example using one of his students—who'd opened her Bible to the exact scripture she was looking for. The same thing I'd done with my journal. He did warn that without proper discernment finding God's will that way wasn't always a good idea.

In that same talk, Dr. Sproul told of the morning he'd run into an acquaintance at a large, crowded central train station in Chicago, and then run into him again later that afternoon. Were both encounters by chance? Or had God planned them?

To answer, he gave an example from 1 Samuel 4-6. Israel had just lost a battle with the philistines, and the elders sent the Ark with the soldiers, hoping it would help find victory. But Israel was again defeated. The Ark was captured and taken back to philistine territories. While it was in their possession, catastrophes and plagues afflicted several of their cities. As a result, they decided to send the Ark back along with a trespass offering. Rather than having a person take it back, they put the Ark in a cart, hooked it to two cows, and let them pull it where they chose. Here's where the story gets interesting. Those cows had just been separated from their calves. Their natural instinct should've been to return to Philistine to find their offspring. Instead, they turned the other direction and went straight to Israel. Chance or providence?

Dr. Sproul discussed the idea that it was God's will to have the Ark returned to His people. And that this passage was a good reminder that our creator, the God of the Universe, is always in control—down to managing cows according to His purpose.

The morning after on *Revive Our Hearts*, Nancy Leigh DeMoss used a story from Joshua 18 to get across the same idea. The Lord instructed Joshua to distribute to the remaining tribes of Israel *by lot* their inheritance of the conquered lands of Canaan. And the drawing of those lots was not by chance but by providence.

Another listener called in to *Politics and Religion* to share he'd been thinking of a certain verse on his way to church and that during the service that particular verse was talked about. He asked Pastor Baxter, "Is this God at work or just mere coincidence?" Baxter responded that God can certainly work that way to get a message across. Like me, the caller had been wondering if that kind of thing happened to anybody else. Baxter responded with a similar story about how a guest pastor he'd invited to preach spoke about the very scripture Baxter had been thinking about.

Pastors and Small-World Phenomena

It was nice to know that pastors have small-world phenomenon experiences too. Another listener called Pastor Baxter asking about his close spiritual experiences with God. In answer, Pastor Baxter cited two personal examples. He'd had a dream about being invited to preach at a church in Lafayette, Louisiana, and later that day, he got a call from that pastor asking him to do just that. Another time, he prayed that a particular evangelist would call and ask him to preach. He got that call too.

Pastor Stewart has experienced personal small-world phenomena as well, and some have tied to me. His sermon "Ghost, Part 1—Empowered" involved a series of events I'd recorded in my journal less than two months earlier. My original entry was called "The Little Lost Boy—a Seer-Like Experience." I'll share it with you in Chapter 12. Two more entries that echoed that directly followed.

For now, let's get back to Pastor Stewart's sermon. He talked about the Holy Spirit being like the wind—which can't be seen but can be felt. As part of the Godhead, the Holy Spirit is a force for good who helps us in our spiritual development. He points us toward Jesus, gives us the power to do things Jesus has called us to do, and deals with us in a powerful, supernatural way.

Pastor Stewart brought up two examples of how the

A God Thing

Holy Spirit had impacted his life. In the hospital after a heart attack, he was only on a vent for a minimal amount of time and had a remarkably quick recovery that his doctors said was rare. He told another story about the time he needed a nice suit to attend an event and one of his staff brought him several, asking if he knew what to do with them. It just so happened one was a perfect fit.

While most people would consider those things coincidences, He saw them as God in the form of the Holy Spirit at work. There are some theologians who think nothing is coincidence and all things happen because of divine providence. I'd like to leave open the idea that coincidences sometimes occur while at other times divine providence steps in.

SHARING FAITH

Like many believers, my Christian walk began with a strong thirst to acquire knowledge, but as time went on, it became important to me to do more. A lot of Christians call this "witnessing." I like to think of it as sharing what I've learned about Jesus and my faith.

One of the first times I shared was at an auto repair shop. While work was being done on my company car, I talked to the shop manager. He asked if I could recommend a good medicine for depression. I did, but then realized his question opened up a great opportunity to share that Jesus was the ultimate answer—not just to depression but to everything. I told the manager that the more I sought Jesus, the more I received revelations from Him. As it became more and more obvious that God was using me in His divine plans and was willing to work with me, the more elated I became. And that gave me a "high" no medicine ever could. I do want to point out that depression medication can be important, and if you're thinking about going off it, you should always discuss that with your doctor first. Everyone is different. This was just my personal experience.

During our talk, I also told the shop manager about the Old Testament prophecies which describe the coming Messiah and how Jesus fulfilled each of them down to the exact detail. I also said that Pastor Baxter had discovered the modern nations in the Bible in Daniel 7. Then I gave the manager a few EndTime Ministries magazines.

Later that afternoon on *Politics and Religion*, Pastor Baxter mentioned that the fulfillment of Bible prophecy is a very effective way to witness. Another small-world phenomenon occurrence since I'd just done that.

Another time I shared my faith was while driving a nurse to Sherman. Normally, I took Mary, but that day she needed a replacement. I picked up Betty in Denison and headed toward Bonham. While en route, we discussed

A God Thing

Christian talk radio and small-world phenomena. For some reason, I decided to bring up the book I'd wedged into the seat next to her. *Classic Christianity* by Bob George had just been given to me the day before by Morris, the son of a home health patient in Ennis. Bob had a church in Carrollton and hosted a radio program by People to People Ministries. I'd been reluctant to take it because I wasn't sure I'd have time to read it, but I hadn't wanted to be rude.

Betty noticed the book before I told her about it. It turned out her boyfriend was connected to that ministry. She was blown away by that small-world phenomenon. I offered the book to her. She was excited to read it, and I was happy it would not go to waste.

On our return trip from Bonham, we listened to Pastor Baxter interview Katherine Albrecht about radio-frequency identification (RFID) technology. This caught Betty's attention. For over a year, she'd been trying to tell people that everyone was being tracked. She didn't know much about the technology, but she had a strong feeling about it. Many people called her paranoid, so hearing from an expert validated her concerns.

That takes me back to Mary, the nurse I normally drove on that route. One day, she, a few coworkers, and I ate at a restaurant in Sherman called A Taste of China. During lunch, we learned that our server was mourning the death of her son who'd been in a motorcycle accident in

Indonesia. As a testament to her strong grief, she'd lost a significant amount of weight. She told me her son had been a good person, that she'd made all the loving sacrifices of a mother for him, and she was not happy with God for taking him. I mentioned a quote from Jesus's Sermon on the Mount. "Blessed are those who mourn, for they will be comforted" (Matthew 5:4). I also quoted Romans 8:28. "And we know that in all things God works for the good of those who love Him, who have been called according to His purpose." Other people at our table chimed in to help comfort her, and someone gave her contact information for a local church.

Around the same time, I found a new radio program. Pastor Bob Coy from Calvary Chapel Church in Ft. Lauderdale, Florida, hosted *Active Word*. He spoke about a book his ministry had published called *My God Story*, where several people inside and outside of the congregation described how God was working with them to bring about changes in their lives. Thinking it sounded like a good reference for witnessing, I ordered a few.

About three weeks later, I returned to A Taste of China and saw that grieving mother again. I gave her a copy of *My God Story*. There was a chapter titled "Living Through Grief" which dealt with a similar story of a mother losing her son through an auto accident. I hoped that helped her. Later, I was able to distribute the book to other people. God was at work with this.

CASES FOR THE EXISTENCE OF GOD

As I learned more about God's Word, my faith continued to grow. All around me, I began to see cases for the existence of God—in the Bible, in history, and through science.

Something that interested me were the one hundred biblical prophecies about Jesus Pastor Baxter pointed out that have all come true. An example found in Genesis 3:15 describes what the Lord said to the serpent after the fall. "And I will put enmity between you and the woman, and between your offspring and hers; he will crush your head, and you will strike his heel." This was fulfilled at Jesus's death on the cross when He takes the keys of sin and death away from Satan and rises again. Discovering that Bible prophecies make sense and appear to be true helped me to see that the rest of the Bible is also true.

A lot of secular history corroborates the truth of the Bible and the existence of God as well. Go read some of the accounts written by first century historian Flavius Josephus if you're curious to find out more. But even when the history seems to be missing, that doesn't mean the events in the Bible didn't happen. Joseph from the Old

Testament—sold into slavery by his brothers and eventually Pharaoh's right-hand man—doesn't show up in any secular books. But there has been a recent discovery of Joseph coins found in the Cairo Museum.

While the Bible reveals God's Word, science reveals God's works. The bulk of science and theology don't actually conflict they complement. What's amazing is that the Bible got much of the science right even though it was written in ancient times while scientific knowledge was practically nonexistent.

After I came to know God, I could no longer accept that our universe happened without an intelligent creator to shape its existence. So, what about the big bang? On Christian talk radio, Pastor Sproul offered his view that it would be impossible for a big bang to randomly create a well-ordered universe. Ironically, in 1927, it was Belgian priest Georges Henri Joseph Édouard Lemaître who first proposed the idea that creation came from a singularity.

In an online sermon, Pastor Stewart said that while something can't evolve from nothing, God could've used the big bang to create the cosmos through intelligent design, making it compatible with scripture.

It's noteworthy that the order of creation in Genesis pretty much follows the scientific community's version. The simpler life forms came first, then the more complex. Many scientists now admit that in light of the complexity of creation, it had to have been intelligently designed.

The human mind, finite in nature, makes it hard to completely understand the concepts of infinity, the size of the universe, or the length of forever. It's hard to believe that the cosmos came out of nothing. It makes more sense that a being who's always existed and will continue to exist forever made it. And that being is God.

Pastor Stewart also gave some astronomy examples. To people of ancient times, the stars seemed to appear to have a finite number of around a thousand—because that was what was visible to the naked eye. But Jeremiah 33:22 says, "I will make the descendants of David my servant and the Levites who minister before me as countless as the stars in the sky and as measureless as the sands on the seashore." That agrees with the fact that there are many more stars invisible to the naked eye.

Psalm 102:25–26 supports the thermodynamics of Earth being in a state of decay. "In the beginning you laid the foundation of the earth, and the heavens are the works of your hands. They will parish, but you remain; they will all wear out like a garment. Like clothing you will change them and they will be discarded."

Isaiah 40:22 touches on Earth science, showing Earth as spherical even though people in biblical times thought it was flat. "He sits enthroned above the circle of the earth, and its people are like grasshoppers. He stretches out the heavens like a canopy, and spreads them out like a tent to live in." According to the proper translation, "circle" refers to a sphere.

The conflict between faith and science often comes from misreading the Bible which describes how things appear, and this is how most inaccuracies can be explained. The language used is not scientific and is from a person's own earthly perspective. Various genres of literature were used in writing the Bible, bringing different rules of interpretation for each unique style. The Hebrew poetry style of Genesis 1 isn't intended to be taken too literally. Written in very broad strokes, the main point is that God created all things. The passage is more concerned with the fact that God made the world then how He did it. Science focuses on the "know-how." Scripture deals with the "know-why." There's no absolute proof for the existence of God, but there's definitely strong evidence. I believe that anyone who seeks God will find Him. So, if that's you, don't be scared to go looking for answers. God isn't afraid of your questions.

A God Thing

Chapter 5

Healing

Now on his way to Jerusalem, Jesus traveled along the border between Samaria and Galilee. As he was going into a village, ten men who had leprosy met him. They stood at a distance and called out in a loud voice, "Jesus, Master, have pity on us!" When we saw them, he said, "Go, show yourselves to the priest." And as they went, they were cleansed. One of them, when he saw he was healed, came back, praising God in a loud voice. He threw himself at Jesus' feet and thanked him—and he was a Samaritan. Jesus asked, "Were not all ten cleansed? Where are the other nine? Has no one returned to give praise to God except this foreigner?" Then he said to him, "Rise and go; your faith has made you well."
Luke 17:11–19

God can and does respond to prayers for healing. I'm not sure why He heals certain people and not others or heals in some situations and not others, but I am sure that one of the ways He shows Himself to us is through that power. As someone who has personally experienced healing, I am grateful and excited to spread the good news.

Public Healing

Catholic priest Father Fernando Suarez claimed he had the gift of healing. Born in the Philippines in 1967, he moved to Canada. Over time, his ability increased, and his ministry grew. He regularly conducted healing Masses, retreats, and missions that were largely attended.

My wife and I attended two of those Masses along with some friends. The first was in Houston in 2008 at the Catholic Charismatic Center. I'd had doubts. But struggling with some knee and back pain, I decided to give it a chance. On the way there, I prayed that if the healing power truly was from Jesus, then I would like to receive it.

Anyone wanting to be healed was told to wait at the front of the church, and I joined the line. Before Father Suarez began, he asked those in attendance to pray before and while he healed each person. He believed that would help amplify the power. As he went down the line laying hands on us one by one, volunteers stood behind us in case anyone felt overwhelmed and passed out. Several people needed that safety net.

When Father Suarez laid his hands on me, I felt an electromagnetic energy flow through my body, the sensation so strong I almost passed out too. Afterward, my pain appeared to be at least partially healed. Others reported similar experiences.

My second healing Mass took place in Mesquite at the Divine Mercy of Our Lord Catholic Church in December 2009. I became a volunteer and got a chance to meet Father Suarez. When I told him about my earlier experience, he was so impressed he requested I send in my testimony along with my picture to be featured in his next international newsletter, which was published in their January 2010 newsletter. Wow, I hadn't expected that. I also didn't expect him to ask me to give a live testimony *right then* before the service started to a crowd of over a thousand. But I agreed, and it went well. I also offered to take videos and stills and help in other ways.

Many people reported healing that day. One person's high blood sugar dropped. Another guy mostly confined to a wheelchair said he was better and walked more than he was usually able to. While I taped the service up on the platform area, I got drowsy and briefly had to lie down. Maybe from the residual healing power?

After Father Suarez finished with the regular attendees, it was our turn as volunteers. This time when he laid hands on me, the electromagnetic energy wasn't as strong, although it did produce some healing effects. Other people didn't experience that energy at all and asked if they needed to go through the line again in order to feel the power. Father Suarez said "feeling" was not necessary to receive the healing, but he did refer to that power as "resting in the spirit." I think, in some cases, "feeling" the healing helps reinforce people's faith. Maybe not feeling it was a test of faith. I believed that might be true for me because I was further along in my walk with Jesus than I'd been at that first service in Houston.

PRIVATE HEALING

I believe Father Suarez's healing Masses were the real deal. But I've also prayed for healing on my own and received it. In 2010, I'd been struggling with a bothersome pain in my right elbow for about a month. My primary care physician had treated it by periodically aspirating fluids from the inflamed area. But even after the fluids had stopped accumulating, I'd still felt pain. The doctor told me that if the treatment didn't get rid of the pain next time, I would have to get an X-ray and be referred to a specialist—which was distressing.

It had never occurred to me to pray about healing until one evening on my way to Bible study. Again, I had doubts about whether praying would do any good. But I decided to try. I expressed my concerns and asked the Lord to heal my elbow. As I closed with "In Jesus's name I pray, Amen," the sharp pain substantially subsided. Over the next few days, my elbow completely healed. If you're a doubter like me and thinking it could've been mind over matter, trust me, it wasn't. I'd tried that too.

I've had prayers answered quickly in other matters, but the way God healed my elbow was a first for me—and it happened without that electromagnetic energy I'd felt at the healing Masses. Receiving instant healing immediately after prayer is still the most miraculous experience I've ever had. And talk about faith building!

The way the Lord responded to my halfhearted, half-disbelieving prayers showed me He knew and understood my hesitations when it came to fully embracing His existence. He clearly wanted to give me strong evidence. I think He also knew that because it had happened on my way to Bible study, I would be excited to share the good news.

Less than two months later, I had a strange dream about the afterlife. I was on a hospital bed or operating table dying. As I ascended into what I thought might be Heaven, colored LED lights indicated a halfway point on a meter. From there, I ended up in a waiting room with other people. My mother sat next to me. A panoramic window separated us from what appeared to be lost souls from Earth. Getting up from my chair, I somehow got their attention—which maybe I wasn't supposed to because the next thing I knew, I was alone in a dark corridor occasionally lit up with dashing LED lights. Then I woke up.

A God Thing

That dream took me back to the doubts I'd had when I'd halfheartedly prayed about healing. It pointed out my half commitment to God and reminded me to be careful about doing things my own way if I wanted to avoid being lost.

God echoed that idea later that morning through Pastor David Hood's sermon "All You Leave Behind." Pastor Hood encouraged us to give up our own paths to trust God's direction and gave a few examples. In Genesis 12:1–3, God told Abraham to leave his family and his past so that he may become the man through whom all families would be blessed. And trusting God's direction, Abraham did. Pastor Hood shared a personal example as well about driving with his family to Las Vegas. In the total darkness of the desert at night, only their headlights helped them see the way. Sometimes we can't see the big picture, but we have to trust that God is good and that He will light the way. "For I know the plans I have for you," declares the Lord, "plans to prosper you and not harm you, plans to give you hope and a future" (Jeremiah 29:11).

That evening, I heard another sermon about Abraham by Pastor D. G. Hargrove. He talked about how Abraham set an example by staying the course God has set for each one of us. Both sermons reinforced the message in my dream not to write my own story, which only ever led me down a dark passageway to nowhere anyway. I'd much rather walk the road God has laid out for me.

About four months after all that reinforcement, I heard Pastor Pete Briscoe on the radio describing what happens when people go to Heaven. It's important to remember he was talking about people who'd already come to Jesus. You can't work your way into Heaven by your actions. You're saved by Jesus's actions. When He died on the cross and you accepted that gift, you were redeemed. The pastor painted a picture of what Heaven looked like based on our obedience to God on Earth. He said that if saved people have tried to live the life that God wanted for them, they get different rewards than those who didn't. Those words added meaning to my dream.

So did a sermon I watched online from Springcreek Church about doubt being part of the process that strengthens faith. Take Thomas, Jesus's disciple, often called doubting Thomas. Jesus was tolerant, patient, and willing to explain things about His return from the dead. And that increased Thomas's faith. It is good that Jesus is forgiving and understanding. It gives me and other believers hope.

Four years later, I was trying to treat a bee infestation in a crack in the wall outside my house, and I fell off an eight-foot ladder. I had seven fractures in my arm and wrist and two in my elbow—the same elbow that God had healed that night on my way to Bible study. I prayed for healing again. This time, there was no instant miracle. My healing process took place through modern medicine. But I believe God was still part of that.

If you're wondering if He couldn't heal this more complicated injury, know that He's not limited in His power. If He'd wanted to, my bones would've been made whole. There were other things going on in my life at the time, and He was dealing with me in those areas. I think He was trying to get a message across that I might not have received if He'd healed me instantly the way He'd done before. I was still grateful that plates, screws, and physical therapy gave me back 100% usage of my arm, elbow, and wrist.

Once on *Politics and Religion*, a caller told Pastor Baxter he'd instantly healed after prayer but said many people thought his healing had been of the devil. Pastor Baxter responded that although the devil and his demons emulate some of God's miracles, if we know who we're praying to and are adequately grounded in the Word, then the miracle we receive is of God. He shared that he'd been healed eight different times after prayer.

When I'd prayed about my elbow and was healed, I knew who I'd been praying to, even sealing my plea with, "In the name of Jesus I pray, Amen." If you're sincere about your prayers, the devil and his demons can't override them. That one singular experience did more than anything else to reinforce my belief in God. Something similar might do the same for you.

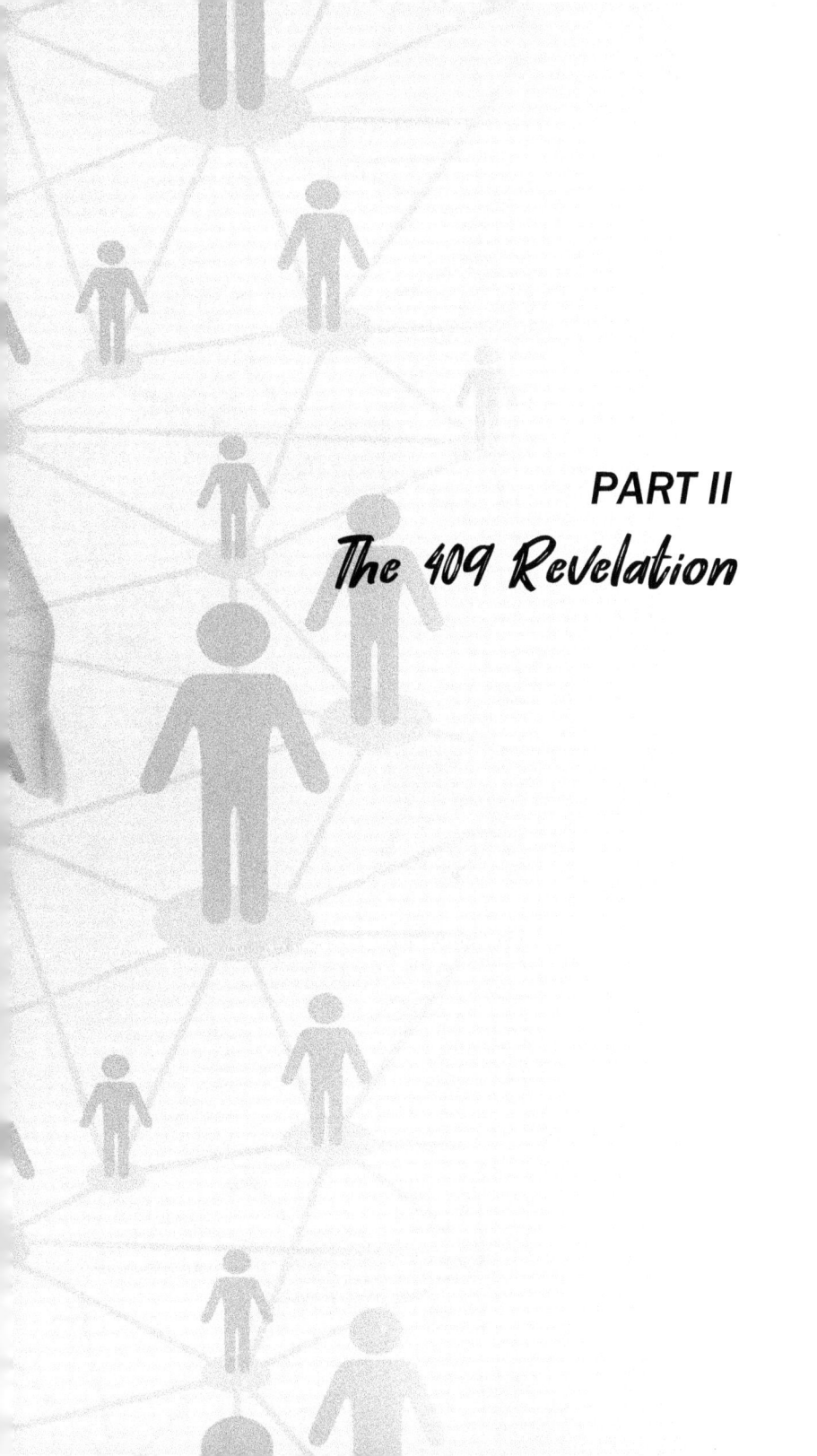

PART II
The 409 Revelation

A God Thing

Chapter 6

Origins of the 409 Revelation

I keep asking that the God of our Lord Jesus Christ, the glorious Father, may give you the Spirit of wisdom and revelation, so you may know Him better.
Ephesians 1:17

I've observed many significant small-world phenomena during my life—especially after I really began paying attention. But there has been one set of connected, reoccurring experiences that led to a major revelation that has had and continues to have a major impact on me. I'll share what I mean over the next several chapters. But I think it's important to start from the beginning.

THE FIRST DATE

I can trace the roots of that revelation to the morning of April 9, 2008. Keep this date in mind as it's the first of two crucial key dates. I'll refer back to it as the original date. That day, I was scheduled to pick up a nurse named

A God Thing

Christina from her house and drive her to visit the home health patients on her schedule. I'd been her driver for a while and had known her even longer.

Let me give you a little backstory. I'd met Christina a few years earlier at my sister Lana's in Richardson. They'd carpooled when they'd both worked at Presbyterian Hospital of Dallas. I eventually bought Lana's house—I'm still there today—and lived down the street from Christina until she moved to Garland.

When I'd first started dating Ghie, I'd brought up Christina because they were both Filipina and I'd needed an icebreaker. Not very creative I know, but it turned out Ghie knew her. They'd gotten acquainted when Ghie had moved to Dallas several years before—a perfect example of a small-world phenomenon in action.

Back to the morning of April 9. When I arrived at Christina's, she told me she'd asked Merna, who owned our home health company, to send her another driver instead. I had ties to Merna beyond work. Also a Filipina, she ran the popular dance group Maharlika that my wife and daughter were in. I sat on their board and was their official videographer for many years.

Disappointed over Christina's request, I stayed in my car puzzled. She hadn't offered an explanation, and the only reason I could come up with was that I'd inadvertently locked the keys in the car last week during one of her patient visits. Because we had a long history of friendship I didn't want to damage, I didn't press her for an explanation.

Starting immediately, Merna swapped my Wednesday schedule with Carlos's. He would be driving Christina, and I would be driving the nurse he usually picked up, Elena—another Filipina.

Halfway through the route that day, Elena and I were waiting at an intersection when her son Billy passed us in her daughter's black Toyota Celica. We'll come back to the significance of that later. Meanwhile, as we were talking, *Politics and Religion* by EndTime Ministries came on the radio. Sometimes I helped Kevin Ritzi, the IT director, video director, and a pastor there with video projects like *Understanding the Bible.* And Kevin helped me on video shoots of Asian and Filipino American events. I told Elena how the connections between EndTime Ministries, the Filipino community—including Merna—and my video projects flowed together.

Earlier, Merna had asked if I could swing by her place after all the patients were seen and I'd taken Elena home. Merna had asked a man over to talk about doing work on her house, and he and his daughter needed a ride home. They lived in my neighborhood, so I'd agreed. As I pulled up by Elena's house to drop her off, I asked if she knew anything about the people I was supposed to pick up. I was

A God Thing

surprised to discover that she did know the man's daughter through a mutual friend and had been there when the daughter and Merna had originally met up at Bistro B, a Vietnamese restaurant in Garland.

That small-world link kept going when I got to Merna's. I knew the daughter too. Her name was Imelda. At that time, she was married to Roger—one of the guys in my EndTime Ministries circle. He was also the guy who'd pointed out the UFOs after Bible study that night. Imelda and Roger both attended North Cities United Pentecostal Church and EndTime University and knew Kevin Ritzi very well. What an amazing connection between so many experiences and so many people.

What had started out as a very disappointing day turned into something special and became one of my greatest prophetic small-world phenomenon experiences. It was a Romans 8:28 thing. God truly does work things out for those who love Him. By refusing to ride with me, Christina had actually done me a huge favor.

THE SECOND DATE

Months later on January 5, 2009—the second key date in the revelation—I drove Elena's son Billy to pay off an outstanding ticket for something he didn't remember. On our way, I told him about what had happened on April 9 and his part in it. When we arrived, the clerk told us the fine was for an unpaid speeding ticket from April 9, 2005. While the year was different from the time his mom and I had seen him at the intersection, it was the same day—April 9. "There's got to be something about April 9," I said to him.

Billy's response was, "409 cleaner." He couldn't explain why that popped into his head. But it made sense to me. April 9 was 4/9 or 4/09. And our purpose there that day was to "clean" up his past to get him back on the right track. Then I had a revelation. Maybe other people involved in the original April 9 events, including myself, were being called by God to clean up our messes too.

Billy's words gave my revelation a name—the 409 Revelation. I consider January 5, 2009, to be what I call a "meaning date"—the first of two—because it gave meaning to the original date April 9, 2008. It also linked them.

The 409 Revelation has turned into a series of interrelated events connected to April 9 that have continued on and become something bigger than itself. I've made over three hundred journal entries of related occurrences for over fourteen years, and they're still ongoing.

Playing with the Numbers

Spotting interesting numerical ties is one of my gifts.

A God Thing

Without going overboard, I'll show you what I mean when it comes to the 409 Revelation. Don't get too lost. Just look for the bigger picture of how the numbers can all be connected.

- 4-9-05 (the date of Billy's speeding ticket)
- 4+5=9 for 2009 (the year Billy named the 409 Revelation)
- 5-4=1 for the date 1-5-09 (January is written as 1 and the day as 5)
- 2009-2005=4 (April can be written as 4— the month that started it all)

About a year after I took Billy to pay his ticket, he ended up in jail for an offense I don't remember. Elena and I visited him there. The inmate number he'd been assigned ties to the 409 Revelation as well.

- Billy's number consisted of 8 digits
- 8=2008 (the original date of the 409 Revelation)
- April 9 is 49 (the last two digits of his number and, interestingly, of my cell)
- 1 and 5 for January 5 (his first and third to last digit for the second key date)
- 100 (his first three digits prompted me to

- count days)
- 94 (the days between key dates January 5 and April 9)
- 49 (If 9 and 4 are flipped)
- 95 (the days apart on a leap year)
- 1 out of 4 years (leap year occurs)
- 94 (rounded down average of 94.25 with leap year)
- 94 (there are 9 months minus 4 days between April 9 and January 5)
- 9 and 4 (constant even during a leap year)

April 9 and January 5 are linked no matter which direction we go. While the above may be a lot to follow, the point is that the numbers reinforce small-world phenomenon events within the 409 Revelation as significant and show that God has a plan for all those tied to it.

I believe God has a plan for everyone. My hope is that you'll discover this for yourself in your own way. Remember, God speaks to us in ways we understand. I love numbers. Maybe that's not your thing. That's okay. God will speak to you in ways that get you excited for Him.

A God Thing

Chapter 7

Anniversaries and Dates

*Count off seven sabbath years—
seven times seven years—
so that the seven sabbath years
amount to a period of forty-nine years.*
Leviticus 25:8

It's interesting to note what pops up on the 409 Revelation timeline. Most noteworthy are the events on every successive April 9 anniversary since 2008. As of now, that's been fourteen years. Some events have also occurred on the anniversaries of related dates, such as January 5. While there are a few I can't share—in order to respect and protect the privacy of others—I can give you the highlights.

THE NUMBER THREE

Three is important to God. The Godhead has three positions—Father, Son, and Holy Spirit. Some people see these as three separate entities, but I tend to believe in one

A God Thing

divine being serving three different roles. Like me in a more earthly example. I'm a father to my daughter, a son to my father, and a husband to my wife. One person. Three roles.

Throughout the Bible, God also uses the concept of the third day to drive His points home. In some instances, the first two days of an event look disastrous while the third comes with a miracle. Jesus died on the cross on day one, stayed in the tomb on day two, but rose on day three. Jonah lived in the belly of a whale days one and two but was freed on day three. When the philistines captured the Ark of the Covenant, God completely turned things around on the third day.

That the number three connects to my small-world phenomena feels like a God thing too. Three became important to the 409 Revelation the day Billy got his speeding ticket on April 9, 2005—three years before the original April 9 date in 2008. Since then, I've discovered anniversary dates that go back and forward in the timeline. I call these prequels and sequels. Most prequel dates show up in three-year increments. Some sequel dates follow that as well, but others are more random.

John S. Lee

April 9 Prequels: Going Back

April 9, 1981

The first event I can link to a prequel anniversary occurred when I was program chairman of the Dallas Divers Club. If you remember, I was also working at Core Labs at the time. I asked John Wisenbaker, the head of Core Labs, to come talk about "The Oil Industry and the Environment." He agreed and spoke on April 9.

The connection between the Dallas Divers and Core Lab began back in October 1975 when I applied for a job there. The first person I was introduced to happened to be the receptionist. I'd met Kay before. She was married to John Cannon, a scuba instructor at a local dive store and the guy who used to work on my car at his house. But I had no idea she worked at Core. A few months earlier, I'd gone on a club trip to Grand Cayman with John's father, Mel, the trip chairman for the Dallas Divers. This might've been a prophetic element to the ongoing link between the club and Core. Quite often, I discover that both my close connections and my strong interests link to 409 Revelation dates as well as to other small-world phenomena in my life.

April 9, 1984

Notice that this next one comes exactly three years after the last. During a Bible study group, I heard about an article *Newsweek* published on April 9 about Germany and

A God Thing

the New World Order Movement. Pastor Baxter discussed it on *Politics and Religion* also, specifically mentioning the date of publication twice. To me, that purposeful repeat was God's way of getting my attention. Like that echo we talked about.

In the *Newsweek* article, the leaders of the New World Order announced their goal to establish a one-world government. It's interesting to note that Germany is one of the modern nations that will be on the Earth during the end times. Pastor Baxter brought up the role of the United States in the end times. He shared that Daniel saw our establishment 2,300 years before it happened. "The first was like a lion, and had eagle's wings. I watched until its wings were plucked off; and it was lifted up from the earth and made to stand on two feet like a man, and a man's heart was given to it" (Daniel 7:4 NKJV). Pastor Baxter believed this scripture described the US breaking away from Great Britain—the lion—to become the independent eagle, which it is.

Several months later, I ran into him and was able to point out that Daniel 7:4 could correlate to a date—July 4 (that can be written as 7-04)—the day the US declared its independence. Soon afterward, he incorporated my input into his lesson plan. It showed up in *EndTime* magazine and on his TV and radio broadcast. I found out later that he continued using my idea after I discovered a DVD set called *Irvin's Last Words*. Words he spoke before he died in November 2020. Thankfully, Pastor Baxter left behind a well-trained and dedicated staff to continue EndTime Ministries and teach Bible prophecy.

As a pastor and teacher, he had a much better grasp of Bible prophecy than I did. But for some reason, God wanted me to reveal to him that Daniel date connection. Much like the 409 Revelation where I had the revelation, but Billy gave it a name. I think this shows just how much God wants everyone to participate in understanding His Kingdom.

April 9, 2002

More recently, I discovered another anniversary. One on which the funeral procession of the Queen Mother, Queen Elizabeth II's mother, fell. That caught my attention because I'd been researching my family tree and found she might be a distant cousin.

On a sidenote—because this event doesn't follow the three-year pattern—I recently noticed that Prince Philip, Queen Elizabeth II's husband, died on April 9, 2021, and that both of those April 9 happenings occurred within the same royal family.

A God Thing

APRIL 9 SEQUELS: GOING FORWARD

April 9, 2009
 I wasn't necessarily expecting anything on that first April 9 anniversary. Yet when it rolled around, I realized that the date occurred over Passover on the day before Jesus was crucified and on the day of the last supper He celebrated with the twelve disciples. That made a total of thirteen men present.

- 4/9 (for April 9)
- 4+9=13

The above alone points the 409 Revelation back to the last supper and to God. But that's not all. Later that evening, I received a text from one of our home health pastors. The date and time stamp? April 9 at 8:49 p.m.

- 8 (for the year of the original date)
- 49 (for 4/9 which is April 9)

It gets better. On April 13, Marlene and I saw patients together, and I shared what had happened with her. When I got to the part where 4+9 = 13, she told me April 13 was a special day for her too. When other people's revelations relate to mine, it's always a reinforcement of what God's trying to tell me. To top it off, we saw thirteen patients that day. I saw thirteen patients with Mary the next day too. All of those things combined established thirteen as an important number within the 409 Revelation.

Years later, I had a conversation with someone on my neighborhood app who mentioned that certain numbers held meaning for her. Out of the blue, I asked if 409 was one of those numbers. Her response was 4+9 = 13. That was pretty cool.

April 9, 2010

Two days prior to the second anniversary of the original April 9 date, I drove a nurse I was rarely assigned to, and we took our lunch break at a Chinese buffet. My fortune cookie read, "Focus on the color purple this week to bring you luck." I then shared the 409 Revelation with her. When we walked toward the register, we saw a bottle of 409 sitting on the shelf—and the numbers were purple.

The numbers on the back of my fortune—4, 9, 19, 22, 32, 45—also grabbed my attention.

- 4 and 9 are obvious
- 22 (means 2 days before the second anniversary)
- 22 (seen on the exit sign off the freeway right after lunch)

A God Thing

Two days later on the actual second anniversary, I told Elena what had happened, and we reminisced about our original experience. I later learned Billy showed up on her porch, much like the prodigal son returning home, after having been lost with no direction or aim for a long time. I don't believe it was a coincidence that he'd played a major role during the formation of the 409 Revelation on April 9, and that he'd returned home on another April 9. Interestingly, he later lived in a halfway house near downtown Dallas right across the street from a bus stop for route 409.

That happens to me a lot. People and things destined to be part of the 409 Revelation come with visible evidence that they belong. That anniversary turned out to be one of the most memorable I've had.

April 9, 2011
Three days before the third anniversary, I had a double three experience. Ironically enough, I'd gotten a traffic ticket. Given the option to take a defensive driving course to "clean up" my record, I signed up for an opening on April 9. Which again brought me back to Billy and the ticket he'd received April 9, 2005, three years before the original April 9, 2008, date. And here I was in 2011, three years after that original date, doing the same with mine. That tied in with the 409 "cleaner" and hit home the idea

God had given me on that first drive with Billy—that the people involved in that original event, including me, might need to clean up our lives. Not surprisingly, some of the students in the course I took discovered they'd experienced small-world phenomena too. God had His hand on that for sure.

April 9, 2013

The most noteworthy event on the fifth anniversary involved a delayed shipment of collectible gold and silver I'd ordered. I had it delivered to my mother's house because I wasn't going to be home.

- The package arrived at 5 p.m. (5 for the fifth anniversary)
- A few minutes before 8:49, I picked it up (a 409 number)

I was tempted to stall until the clock actually hit 8:49 before I opened the package. But since I knew God wanted everything tied to the 409 Revelation to come from Him, I figured He might not appreciate my manipulation. So, I didn't wait.

As soon as I removed the contents, a packet filled with mercury silver dimes broke.

A God Thing

- 8:49 was the time the dimes scattered all over
- 498 was the total count when I collected them (the original April 9 date)

I still have those coins safely tucked inside my safety deposit box. Completely out of my control, this event was significant in establishing Who is in control. God, not me. That supported the idea that I shouldn't try to script my own life. Drafting my story was better left up to Him.

April 9, 2015
On the seventh anniversary, FOX News did a story about the 2013 Boston marathon bombing. In the video, they showed a video at the finish line.

- 4:09 was the elapsed race time on the clock when the bomb went off

May 1, FOX brought it up again. This time, the video zoomed in on the clock.

- 4:09:51 was the elapsed time down to the seconds (5/1 is the news story date)
- 5/1 (May 1 is the reverse date of January 5 if you flip the calendar numbers)

April 9, 2016

I had two video projects to record funerals for Filipino families scheduled on the eighth anniversary, something that never happened. Video and the Filipino community had both helped me discover some of the original interconnections within the 409 Revelation. Also right before I went to bed that night, the date and time on my watch linked me personally to the 409 Revelation.

- 4-9-16 was the date on my watch
- 12:07 was the time (12 for December and 7 for the day of my birthday)

FLIP-SIDE DATES

We have the two calendar dates that link to the 409 Revelation—April 9 and January 5. But other dates connect as well. I call them "flip-side" or "reverse" dates because you flip the calendar numbers. April 9 (4/09) becomes September 4 (9/04). January 5 (1/05) becomes May 1 (5/01). You saw this above with May 1 in the story on the Boston marathon bombing.

September 4, 2013

On this flip-side date to April 9 (4/09), I drove behind a car with the license plate 949 and saw those numbers as the flip-side dates (9/04) to April 9 for the first time.

A God Thing

September 4, 2014

Exactly a year later, I saw 494—a reversal—on another license plate. Remember when I mentioned there were 94 days between the two key dates January 5 and April 9?

JANUARY 5 ANNIVERSARY DATE

January 5, 2015

Although nothing earth-shattering usually happens on January 5 anniversaries, 2015 was an exception. I asked my friend Warren to help me pick out and install two water faucets in my bathroom. At the store, we were both drawn to a particular model.

- C49 was the shelf where we found them (49 for the 409 Revelation)
- $48.00 was the price (48 for April 2008)

There'd been only two faucets left—the exact number I needed—which was another sign I should buy them. Heading toward the checkout, I glanced at my watch. It was close to 4:09. But like with the coins, I didn't try to rig the receipt to have a 4:09 time stamp. But that didn't mean I wasn't hoping for it to happen.

At the self-checkout, something went wrong printing the receipt. The clock passed 4:09. A store employee printed it out for me at the central register instead—and it read January 5, 2015, at 4:09 p.m. The 15 for the year further reinforces January 5.

January 5, 2016
A year later to the day, I opened an email from SpeeDee Oil Change and Auto Service announcing a chance to win four tickets to the biggest race of the year that happened to be on . . . April 9. Something else that linked January 5 and April 9 together in a setup I believe God knew would get my attention.

THE NEGATIVE SIDE TO THE 409 REVELATION

As my early 409 experiences were all positive, I didn't expect anything different moving forward. A work Christmas luncheon in 2012 changed that. During a 409 Revelation conversation with Marsha, one of the nurses, told me April 9 had been the worst day of her life. It was the day she'd gotten married back in 1993, and the marriage had been nothing short of a disaster. I think that discussion happened because God wanted me to be prepared for some negativity and conflict when it came to my revelation.

During a tour of the Nimitz World War II Museum in Fredericksburg, I discovered April 9, 1942, to be the day US forces under the command of General King were forced to surrender the Philippines. You already know my connection there.

German pastor Dietrich Bonhoeffer was also killed on April 9, 1945, for speaking out against anti-Christian activities. The Gestapo murdered him with piano wire. And if you'll notice, these two events happened three years apart on the prequel timeline.

Even before I discovered these things, I was beginning to see that not everything connected to 409 events would turn out well, including some personal interactions. I believe it was Pastor Keith who once pointed out in a sermon that affinity is not always the best path to friendship. It can help. But alone, it isn't always enough. I've had several acquaintances with much in common, yet we still found ourselves at odds.

December 7

December 7 is the third key date of the 409 Revelation—and the second meaning date—because it brings more meaning to April 9, which started the events. January 5 gave the events a name and the idea that we're supposed to clean things up, both physically and spiritually. December 7 became the barometer that showed that all things 409 aren't meant to be good or bad—they just are. And earlier, I mentioned that it connected me to the revelation though my birthday.

It's interesting that December 7 contains God numbers. December is the twelfth month. There are twelve months in a year. And twelve is the number of God's government and the number of Jesus's disciples. As far as seven goes, it's God's number of completion. There are seven days in a week. But on the other side, the bombing of Pearl Harbor also occurred on this date. Where God likes to put his name, so does the devil.

December 7, 2013
I stumbled across a TV show that, like the conversation with Marsha, opened my eyes to see that everything in the 409 Revelation wasn't always going to be positive. The scene I caught happened to show a truck erratically weaving through traffic, fishtailing, and then wrecking. The police called to the scene mentioned specifically that April 9, 2008, was the worst day of their lives. That blew me away as it tied this day, December 7, to the original April 9 date and established it as the third most important date in the revelation.

December 7, 2020
I experienced several events on a trip to Durant, Oklahoma. The one that stood out occurred at Choctaw Casino. I walked to the movie theater's digital billboard to see the movie choices, and the time read 4:09—another

A God Thing

thing that linked December 7 and my birthday to the 409 Revelation.

DECEMBER 7 AND THIS BOOK

December 7 is the date God used—three times on two different occasions—to get His message across for me to write this book. In November 2020, I made the commitment to rewrite the first two chapters, then continue until I completed the manuscript. At that point, the time that had elapsed from the original April 9 came out to twelve years and seven months (12/7). Sometimes it amazes me how God uses numbers that interconnect events to get my attention and show me things He wants me to see.

Do you have any dates in your life that seem significant? Can you see any patterns connected to them? Perhaps this is your sign to take a closer look at meaningful dates in your life to see whether there might be a connection you didn't realize was there.

Chapter 8
Celestial Symmetry

When I consider your heavens, the work of your fingers,
the moon and the stars, which you have set in place,
what is mankind that you are mindful of them,
human beings that you care for them?
Psalm 8:3–4

Several years back, I discovered the vertical ribbon on a globe. If you've never noticed it before either, it shows the position of the sun as it corresponds to all the dates of the year. Not knowing much about that ribbon, I researched it online.

It's called a solar analemma. And it has to do with where the sun is seen each day—from a fixed location, at the exact same time, without daylight savings time interfering so the data doesn't get skewed. The ribbon indicates the sun's position using altitude and azimuth. Altitude refers to the vertical measurement and azimuth to the horizontal. The average dates for the equinoxes and solstices are:

A God Thing

- spring equinox (March 21)
- summer solstice (June 22)
- fall equinox (September 23)
- winter solstice (December 22)

I'm not sure how these dates are determined, and they can vary depending on the source, but they work out perfectly for what I want to share.

Something—maybe God—prompted me to look at the relationship between April 9 and September 4. I discovered April 9 is nineteen days after the spring equinox, and September 4 is nineteen days before the fall equinox. That places the sun at almost the same altitude on both dates. I call this celestial symmetry.

I also noticed something similar between the two key 409 Revelation meaning dates. January 5 is 14 days after the winter solstice, and December 7 is fifteen days before. January 5 is seventy-five days before the spring equinox, and December 7 is seventy-five days after the fall equinox.

Other 409 dates have symmetry too but not based on the sun's position. October 9 and 12 are noteworthy. We'll talk about why later. But for now, I want to point out that the October dates are roughly six months apart from April 9, and their symmetry puts the Earth on the opposite side of its orbit. April 9 is nineteen days after the spring equinox, and October 12 is nineteen days after the fall equinox.

September 4 and October 12 are nineteen days before and after the fall equinox. That all these dates have celestial tie-ins is yet another reason why the 409 Revelation must be a God thing.

A few years after reading about the solar analemma, something else caught my attention. NASA learned that the Voyager 1, a space probe they'd launched in the '70s, had ventured beyond our solar system's heliosphere—the spherical area of solar magnetic fields that circles the sun. This means Voyager 1 reached a part of space where the influence of our solar system on the probe became less than the influence of interstellar space. If you're curious, you can go to NASA's site (nasa.gov) to learn more. The best part—and why it matters here—is that NASA made this discovery on April 9, 2013. The date adds to the celestial tie-ins of the 409 Revelation and shows that it goes beyond the Earth and Sun to include a wider slice of the heavenly realms.

On a sidenote, there's something worth mentioning beyond my small-world phenomena and the 409 Revelation. It involves two winter solstices witnessed by millions of people set ten years apart—2010 and 2020—which both mark a new decade.

The first was a lunar eclipse that hadn't been seen for hundreds of years during a winter solstice. When it was happening, the moon had a reddish color with an amber tint—a blood moon. A blood moon was also observed during Jesus's crucifixion.

The second was the proximity of Jupiter and Saturn. The two planets came so close together they could be seen with the naked eye as a single bright star. The same thing had happened four hundred years ago but during the day, which made it hard to observe. But eight hundred years ago, the event occurred at night. There are some who say perhaps this was the star of Bethlehem that led the three wise men to Jesus. Jesus was born during the winter solstice close to the darkest time of the year in the Northern Hemisphere. Some believe that star to be the symbolism that showed God bringing light into the world as well as pointing the way for the three wise men to find Jesus. It's also interesting that both December 7 and January 5 are near the winter solstice. I believe that's a testimony that God has His signature all over it.

Have you observed anything that shows you God's signature? I believe you only have to look to find the many ways He displays His handiwork.

Chapter 9

Formula 409 Cleaner

> *Blind Pharisee!*
> *First clean the inside of the cup and dish,*
> *and then the outside will be clean.*
> *Matthew 23:26*

Remember that bottle of 409 I spotted during my lunch at the Chinese buffet? Let's come back to that so I can show you how it's connected to my 409 Revelation story.

BEFORE THE DISCOVERY

In October of 2011, I got off work in time to attend Occupy Dallas. Inspired by Occupy Wall Street—a movement set on righting social and economic injustice—the local event was organized by radio host Alex Jones and drew lots of protesters to the Federal Reserve.

As a videographer, I wanted to take video and stills. I got some great footage of Alex speaking into a megaphone

A God Thing

about how the Federal Reserve wasn't owned by the federal government but instead by private banks. Most of my coverage centered on what he had to say about the "Private Property No Trespassing" sign in front of the building. I just happened to be in the right position to pan over to it as he made his argument. Simply put, he pointed out that if the Federal Reserve was truly federal and not private, it belonged to the citizens and shouldn't display a sign that said, "Private Property." His speech got a lot of views on YouTube, and when I returned to the same spot several months later, that sign was suspiciously absent.

Not long after the event, I turned on *The Alex Jones Show* to an interview with local financial expert Dan Cofall. In addition to hosting his own radio show, *The Wall Street Shuffle*, he was co-chairman and CFO of NorAm Capital Holdings, Inc. and CEO and president of NorAm Media Group, Inc. Dan said he'd been at Occupy Dallas and praised Alex's speech and the way he'd handled his argument. This made me glad I'd filmed Occupy Dallas and inspired me to share it on YouTube.

With a little editing, I put together a coherent short story of the event. It took about three months and was my first and last attempt to upload a video to YouTube. If you're interested, you can watch "Alex Jones at the Federal Reserve" on my YouTube channel, 409Revelation. I've included a link at the end of the book. After I posted the video, I sent an email and the link to a select group of people, including Dan Cofall since he was very much a part of the story.

The next day I got a response from Dan. He said what I'd written and filmed was interesting and well-chronicled. Then he asked about the "409" in my YouTube channel name. He was curious because NorAm was formed back in 1960, and its original product was Formula 409 cleaner. Wow! That connected Dan with my 409 Revelation world. And the fact that I named my channel prior gave it a prophetic feel.

Unlike me, Dan saw the name as an interesting coincidence, not divine providence. Nevertheless, it still caught his attention. Which proved that even though people don't always see things the way I do, they're still fascinated by small-world phenomena. I think events become more interesting when we realize they might be more than coincidences.

With Dan Cofall linked to Alex Jones, I discovered a 409 Revelation connection to Alex as well not three months later. In the past, people in my church used to kid me about Alex, teasing me that they'd seen him wearing a 409 shirt on TV, when they definitely hadn't. I'd ignored it until I found a real connection. Then I had the last laugh. On his show, Alex shared an interesting experience. He'd been in church on a day with less than a hundred in attendance and only a handful of kids. Two of the kids had physical health issues. One was in a wheelchair. Alex was thinking of hugging this boy, but something stopped him that he said he believed was the Holy Spirit. A feeling came over him that the boy and his family would come up to him instead after church and let him know they listened to his radio show. He also got a glimpse of some of the other things they would talk about. And that's exactly what happened! It was the first time Alex shared a spiritual small-world phenomenon experience somewhat similar to my 409 Revelation happenings. And get this—he said it on April 9, 2012.

THE ORIGINS OF FORMULA 409

Formula 409 was invented in 1957 by Morris D. Rouff as a commercial solvent and degreaser for industries with difficult cleaning issues. NorAm Capital Holdings, Inc., formally known as Harrell Hospitality Group, Inc., was incorporated in 1959 under the name Formula 409, Inc. and purchased the rights to the product from Rouff. The founding partners—Wilson Harrell, David Woodcock, and Art Linkletter—were eventually bought out by Clorox.

Brian Rouff, the inventor's son, claims the 409 name came from his mother's birthday—April 9. Ruth's date of birth fits the narrative of my 409 Revelation story. Clorox claims the name came from the four hundred and nine test runs they did before the right formula was found. But there was no reason for Brian to lie. Which makes me believe there's something more to this story. But either way, the name works for me.

Additional Interconnections

My 409 story continued to deepen, especially after a personal encounter with Art Linkletter, one of the original partners. On October 9, 2005, Mark, an old associate, invited me to be a subcontractor at a medical convention in The Woodlands, Texas. As a second source to lead producers Durum Video and Opossum Trotter Productions, I set up about twenty feet from Art Linkletter to help tape his interview.

It's interesting that I met Art two-and-a-half years before April 9, 2008—six months after Billy received his speeding ticket. Coincidence? Maybe. But as another type of a celestial symmetry sign, I believe it was so much more and that God was involved.

Recently, I discovered something else that connects to the 409 Revelation and to Art Linkletter. Bear with me as I set it up, then I'll show you how it ties together. I had started watching *Supernatural*. The TV series is about two

A God Thing

brothers, Dean and Sam Winchester, who hunt demons, ghosts, vampires, and other monsters all over the United States. In a Season 1 episode called "Hell House," they traveled to Richardson, Texas—the suburb of Dallas where I've lived for nearly thirty years.

I mentioned it to my daughter and son-in-law, Trent. Trent showed me on his phone that Jensen Ackles, the actor who plays Dean, graduated from Berkner in Richardson less than a mile from me where Trent, Alyssa, and my nephew Scott also graduated. Jensen attended Dartmouth Elementary School and Apollo Jr. High in my neighborhood too. I wonder if I'd ever seen him as a kid. What a very cool small-world phenomenon.

A few months later in Season 5, there was an episode with a conversation between Dean and the Archangel Michael about the importance of the Winchester bloodline. Michael said it dated back to the days of Cain and Abel and the Winchester family tree was predestined and didn't come about through random chance. Dean's response included something about the Kevin Bacon Factor—another element to the six degrees of separation involving Kevin's connections to actors and acting projects. Something similar was repeated in the next episode. The time stamp showed it was said at fifteen minutes and forty-nine seconds. This represents January 5 (1/5 for 15) and April 9 (4/9 for 49). What a 409 Revelation reinforcement.

Back to where Art Linkletter fits in. Not long before I watched those episodes of *Supernatural*, I'd looked up stuff about Art Linkletter. Pictures and articles popped up. But so did a picture of Jensen as Dean Winchester—with his character's name written across the image. Why that showed up, I'm not sure. But clearly it was a link between me, Jensen Ackles, and Art Linkletter. I was never able to make that happen again in a search. Could it have been supernatural? Maybe. Maybe not. But I do know I was meant to see that image. I think God was at work here. Can you see places where He's at work in your life as well?

A God Thing

Chapter 10

People and Things

*He is before all things,
and in Him all things hold together.
Colossians 1:17*

As time goes on, I seem to come across more and more connections to the 409 Revelation. These links continue to surprise me every time I find them. I have no doubt that God wants to make it clear that both small-world phenomena and the 409 Revelation are real in my world. I appreciate that He knows that numbers and patterns get my attention and uses them to constantly remind me what He thinks is important.

PEOPLE

During my time as the official videographer of the Asian American Texas Pageant, I met Angie Chen Button. As one of the judges, she already had ties to some of the Asians and Filipino Americans interconnected to the 409

A God Thing

Revelation.

I reintroduced myself to Angie in 2008 when she first ran for Texas State Representative in District 112 of the Texas Legislature where I live. She won that election and many after.

For quite some time, I'd been involved with her campaigns, worked on her team, and participated in her constituent roundtables. A popular representative, her name can be found near the top of the "best" list in *Texas Monthly's* article "2021: The Best and Worst Legislators." It's said she chooses to act rather than speak, doesn't show off or upstage her louder colleagues, and serves in the legislature in a no-drama style.

Back in February 2010, I read an article in *The Dallas Morning News* by Robert T. Garrett. "How Washington Became The Issue" was about then Governor Rick Perry getting behind sophomore legislator Brandon Creighton who supported a states' rights resolution. A picture showed the two men along with three other state congressional members, including Angie Chen Button—a freshman legislator at the time. The press conference took place on April 9, 2009.

Ten years later, I participated in many roundtable topic discussions, including Urban Affairs, a committee Angie chaired. Some people at my church invited me to share the committee's position on a particular bill (HB

1257) surrounding a controversial issue. As they represented a different side of the argument, I became kind of a liaison between them and Angie's team.

One of the things they wanted was to set up a meeting with Angie and/or her staff in Austin. When they reached out, the only day that worked for her happened to be April 9. I don't see that as a coincidence but as a pretty clear 409 Revelation occurrence. Unfortunately because of a conflict, that meeting was canceled and not rescheduled. But the fact that April 9 was the only date Angie had considered validates that 409 connection. And more than that, the time stamp on the cancelation email was 12:57—which corresponded to HB 1257.

On April 9, 2021, I received an invite to attend a virtual roundtable. That made thirteen years of 409 Revelation events in a row on the original April 9 anniversary. I attended the meeting via Zoom. When I glanced at the number in attendance, it was fifteen—representing January 5 and solidifying the connection.

Many years ago, I was associated with a community church group from North Cities United Pentecostal Church, which included EndTime Ministries. We called our group the Tea Party Brethren. One of the members had an aunt with an April 9 birthday. Another had a phone number with the last four digits 9409. If you remember, 94 represents the reverse of April 9, and the 409 is obvious.

A God Thing

The last four digits of my phone number at the time were 7749. If you take 7 X 7, you get 49, and 49 and 409 are interchangeable.

OTHER CONNECTIONS

Out of curiosity, I once did a Google search on things associated with the number 409. Most of the results that came up were ones I'd expected.

One of the first things to pop up was Chevy's 409 engine, including several different models of the 1963 and 1964 Impala. At the time, it was said that the 425 hp Turbo-Fire 409 cubic inch V8 could be tucked into any 1964 Chevrolet.

Reading about the 409 engine reminded me of an article in the November 29, 2009, issue of the *Dallas Morning News* about Charles Nearburg. "Racing to be World's Fastest Driver" covered the Dallas oilman and racer at the Bonneville Salt Flats in Utah where he was on a "quest" to beat the current land speed record. Guess what that record was? You're right if you said 409 mph. On a sidenote, this also ties to Dan Cofall who had a strong interest in racing cars.

I read the Nearburg story on November 30, 2009, while out with a home health nurse. Our patient had a 406 address, but the house I faced across the street when I parked was 409. The 409 is obvious. The 406 is also relevant if you look at the significant date of January 5 as 1+5=6. Those discoveries were enough to declare that date in 2009 a 409 Revelation day.

Other items that showed up in my search were the Beach Boys song "409," New Balance 409 cross trainers, an electronics shop in Hong Kong, and the website www.409shop.com. A few people had posted as well, saying the number had meaning to them. And it seemed relevant to other organizations that weren't directly connected to my 409 Revelation too.

I already mentioned *Numb3rs* and its small-world phenomenon, but I also discovered ties from the show to the 409 Revelation. Season 1, Episode 8, *Identity Crisis* is about reopening an old case because of a wrongful conviction. The number 8 represents 2008, the original year of the April 9 happening. At fifteen minutes in, an FBI agent asks a murder suspect, "Where were you on April 9, 2004?" The fifteen minutes represents January 5. It's interesting that the 2004 date in that episode was exactly one year before Billy got his speeding ticket. Another quote from the episode stated, "There was a 4.9 % chance that the same MO being used on two different victims by two different killers was a coincidence." And you won't be surprised when I say 4.9 represents 409.

In June of 2022, this April 9, 2004, date cropped up

A God Thing

on *Criminal Minds*. In Season 9, Episode 13, "The Road Home," Dr. Spencer Reid calculated in his head the original date of an event being investigated by the Behavior Analysis Unit (BAU) team. This also contained 409 revelation numbers, like the season and episode numbers. And both FBI characters from each show were geniuses in many subjects, including math. How about that! This is another double reinforcement like the others you've seen in this book.

In Episode 19 of Season 10, "Beyond Borders," we see April 9 again when a family is killed on vacation in 2004 by the fifteen-year-old son who'd been abused by his father. The murder happened on April 9—the father's birthday—which is what triggered the massacre. The son's age represents January 5. The fact that I watched this episode seven days after the other episode—7 being the square root of 49—reinforces the connection.

ALDI, my favorite neighborhood grocery store, is less than half a mile from my house. The prices are reasonable, and it's very convenient. The street address is 1549, an obvious 409 Revelation number. Many times when I've gone there, I've received receipts where the time stamp includes 409 numbers.

I've also encountered other number combinations that remind me of the 409 Revelation. One is 1+5=6. This is a January 5 total, like 4+9=13, and is significant to April 9.

When 6 and 13 are added together, the sum comes out to 19. The third most important date in the 409 Revelation is December 7, in which 12+7 also equals 19. Interesting, isn't it?

The twelfth anniversary of the original 409 happening was April 9, 2020. That day I felt pressure to get some things done and happened to look at my watch—only to discover the time was 4:09:20. That paralleled the date.

I decided to jump back on Google again to search for more things on the 409 Revelation and see if anyone else thought the numbers had a personal meaning to them. My 409 Revelation turned out to be unique to me, but special bicycle parts that dealt with shock absorbers did pop up. The most pronounced models were "Fork Rock Shox Revelation 409 2008 oil value levels" and "Rock Shox Revelation 409 released in 2009," two separate models that operate differently. Note that the years 2008 and 2009 mentioned above are in line with my 409 Revelation. To anyone else, this might be a coincidence. Not to me.

I also got a biblical result for Revelation 409. While there's no Chapter 409, there is a Revelation 4:9. It states, "Whenever the living creatures give glory, honor and thanks to Him who sits on the throne and who lives for ever and ever." The chapter discusses the throne in Heaven, and I think verse 9 is a bridge statement between the four living creatures and the twenty-four elders who give glory, honor, and thanks to Jesus. I would say this points to Jesus Christ and gives yet another clue that my 409 Revelation comes from God.

Other 4:9 verses that stood out through listening to sermons or Christian talk radio are below.

- Genesis 4:9: "Then the Lord said to Cain, 'Where is your brother Abel?'" In this question of brotherly love, we're to take care of each other. Love your brother, love others, and you will love God.
- Matthew 4:9: "All this I will give you," he said, "if you will bow down and worship me." During Jesus's time fasting in the desert, Satan offered Him the kingdoms of the world—an offer He rejected to follow God's plan. This reminded me of that dream I'd had back in the '90s.
- John 4:9: "The Samaritan woman said to Him, 'You are a Jew and I am a Samaritan woman. How can you ask me to drink?' (For Jews do not associate with Samaritans)." Jesus broke traditional barriers to include everyone with everlasting living water.
- 1 John 4:9: "This is how God showed His love among us: He sent His one and only Son into the world that we might live through Him." Jesus

loved all of humanity.

The last two scriptures were written by John and have significant meaning to me. My name is also John, and that draws me directly into the 409 Revelation connection.

I recently learned through an online sermon by Pastor Stewart that the whole Gospel of John encompasses additional 409 Revelation connections. It contains seven groupings of seven in regard to Jesus. Remember that seven is a number that refers to completion or perfection when it comes to God. John is a numbers guy and deliberately uses numbers favorable to God to reinforce his messages. You can find seven signs of miracles that Jesus presented, seven "I am" statements, seven witnesses who testify of Jesus, seven ministries of the Holy Spirit, seven life-changing conversations of Jesus, seven women involved in the storytelling, and seven questions Pontius Pilate asks Jesus.

John also used the number three. He made a point to mention that the wedding where Jesus performed the miracle of turning water into wine happened on the third day of the week. He did this to emphasize the day of deliverance, which parallels to when promises of God came to fruition. One example is that Jesus rose on the third day. Both seven and three are connected to the 409 Revelation.

A God Thing

Here's another 4:9 scripture I stumbled onto. "Whatever you have learned or received or heard from me—put it into practice. And the God of peace will be with you" (Philippians 4:9). This means we're to do what we know. We need to move beyond hearing the Word and act on the Word. That's when we'll find peace.

This mirrors the meaning of the 409 Revelation that I learned on January 5, 2009, and can be interpreted as one of the things that each of us can clean up in our lives. Once we know what it is that God wants us to do, we shouldn't ignore it but act on it to the best of our ability. This allows Him to work in our lives.

Have you ever noticed that "Philippians" sounds a lot like "Philippines"? Many Filipinos are part of the 409 Revelation. Another link in my life.

Think about your life. What is God telling you? Is He putting things in front of you that might not be coincidences? Is He trying to get your attention? Take the time to find out. You won't be sorry you did. I'm not. I love discovering the new ways He's speaking to me.

Chapter 11

Sandy the Dolphin and Scuba Diving

*So God created
the great creatures of the sea and every living thing
with which the water teems and moves about in it,
according to their kinds,
and every winged bird according to its kind.
And God saw that it was good.*
Genesis 1:21

The day after Thanksgiving way back in 1976, I had a very cool meet and greet with a wild dolphin at San Salvador Island in the Bahamas. That year was the bicentennial of the birth of the United States. That island was where Christopher Columbus was widely believed to have first landed in the New World on October 12, 1492. Isn't that combination exciting? It was to me. I'm sure you've figured out by now how much I love it when events and dates and places connect together.

A God Thing

SANDY

I went to San Salvador Island on a week-long scuba trip with a group from Dallas. The dives were amazing—full of sea life, colorful corals, and clear water. On the hunt for interesting creatures, I ended up taking a lot of underwater photographs. The last day of the final dive, I got separated from my dive buddy and missed the hammerhead shark others saw a hundred feet down.

But I found something better about ten feet from the surface when a wild Bottlenose dolphin swam right up to greet me. Maybe to protect me from the shark? Or maybe because it had just been in the area? Either way, I welcomed the opportunity. And thanks to the dolphin shows I'd seen on TV, I wasn't afraid.

Friendly but cautious, the dolphin wouldn't allow me to touch it, but it did let me stay close—within about two feet—and take photos. After we swam together for about ten minutes, I returned to the dive boat and told the other divers. Eager to get close to a dolphin as I'd been, they jumped into the water and swam with it too. Everyone who shared that experience—and even those who just heard about it—seemed blown away. At that time, running into a wild dolphin was rare. And to be the first person to interact with that dolphin, who was later named Sandy, was an amazing experience. For over a year after that, swimming with Sandy became a treat for any visiting diver.

Back in those days, as a young adult, I lacked self-assurance and wasn't very accomplished. God knew that. Which is why I believe He didn't just orchestrate such a special meeting, He also let me be the one to encounter Sandy first during that dive. Being first gave me a little fame—something I don't seek out. I'm not that type of person. I think this was His way to encourage me and help me build confidence. It worked.

Sandy became the catalyst that catapulted my interest in both scuba diving and underwater photography. Twenty years later, I started a video production company and named it Dolphin Productions. I still have that business today.

SANDY'S 409 REVELATION CONNECTIONS

A few years ago, during a search for something to help out my friend Paul with a past project I'd shot, I stumbled across a DVD of the movie *Day of the Dolphin*. The record date was 4-9-07—exactly one year before the original April 9, 2008, date. That's just one thing that links Sandy with the 409 Revelation.

Earlier, I mentioned Christopher Columbus landed on San Salvador Island on October 12. That date shares six-month celestial symmetry with April 9. Another link.

A God Thing

When I drove nurses to see patients, we'd routinely exit I-30 at Dolphin Road. The exit number was 49B. And 49, of course, represents April 9. Also if the B isn't written clearly, it could be seen as an 8 or a 13, which are both 409 Revelation numbers. Many times on Dolphin Road, I saw other 409-type signs, like the cost for gas being $4.09 a gallon. Numbers like that crept up for years.

They still do. In March of 2021, my wife and I left Fair Park in Dallas, the exit we had to take directed us to Dolphin Road, I-30, and exit 49B. At Haskell and Dolphin, the corner gas station advertised gas for $2.49 a gallon. The 2 is for the second turn we took to get there, and the 49 is obvious. I also noticed that we were at the 4900 block of Dolphin Road. To me, this points out how 409 Revelation happenings stand the test of time and why I believe they're a God thing.

Other mile markers tie in as well. I'll talk more about the 409 marker along I-35E below. After I began looking, I found a 409 time stamp more than once as I crossed it. The same thing happened at exit 49 along Highway 75N.

NEW BRAUNFELS SCUBA DIVING TRIPS

Since the '70s, I've been taking one or two trips a year to Central Texas to snorkel in the San Marcos and Comal

Rivers. Until recently, I owned a large lot in nearby Canyon Lake, also a good place for scuba diving. I look forward to these trips. In certain places, the spring fed waters can exceed more than thirty feet of visibility and have a variety of aquatic plant and animal life to enjoy.

During my 2019 trip, I noticed a silver alert from New Braunfels on a highway sign on I-35E close to mile marker 409. The man had a similar height and weight as mine, and his age, 86, was the reverse of mine, 68. In other places in this book, you've seen where number reversal has shown some significance. Was this more than an interesting coincidence? I think it was.

As I got closer to New Braunfels, I saw a different silver alert about a car that was last seen in Richardson—where I lived and where I began my trip. When I finally arrived at the Heidelberg Lodges in New Braunfels where I always stay, I went to the Comal River. At the edge was a cement walkway with a ladder. From the top of it to the surface of the water, it was four inches. The San Marcos River had a similar cement walkway and ladder. That same day, it had a measurement of nine inches. That's 4 and 9—another 409 Revelation indication.

My 2020 trip also involved some 409 occurrences. Because of construction, I wasn't able to see mile marker 409 as I headed south, but I did see the highway sign that had flashed the silver alert. It was eight miles north of where the marker would normally be, and eight represents the original 409 year.

At mile marker 349, I happened to look at my watch. It was 8:49 a.m. As I've shown, three is a significant number in my 409 world. And, of course, the 4, 9, and 8 represent April 9, 2008. The time and mile marker both having a 4 and 9 highlights the interconnectivity.

After I checked into the Heidelberg, I again measured the water levels at both rivers. The San Marcos showed fifteen inches and the Comal River nine. This is another 409 Revelation thing going back to the second most important date, January 5, 2009. That was two times in a row with two different ways to connect.

Two days later on my return trip, I passed mile marker 409 at exactly 3:49 p.m. In military time, that's 15:49 which is a reinforcer along with the mile marker 349 and 8:49 time I'd seen on the way down. 409 Revelation events keep cropping up in things I do frequently.

Do you have similar experiences with events and dates and places that continue to link together and build on each other? Start watching for them. Maybe God's trying to point something special out to you too.

Chapter 12

Why Me?

*In the last days, God says,
I will pour out my spirit on all people.
Your sons and daughters will prophesy,
your young men will see visions,
your old men will dream dreams.
Even on my servants, both men and women,
I will pour out my spirit in those days, and they will prophesy.
Acts 2:17–18*

One Sunday, Pastor Stewart mentioned Joseph of Arimathea in a sermon. A close relative of Jesus, Joseph assumed responsibility for Jesus's burial after the crucifixion. Through Solomon, Joseph descended from King David. From there, his line eventually continued on in Ireland, Scotland, and England. Pastor Stewart thought there was a chance he'd come from that lineage. Excited to discover that I might also share that ancestry, I decided to get on the computer in my bedroom and shoot him an email.

In the middle of writing that email, a strange almost catlike sound came from outside my window. A minute later, it returned more clearly. But this time, it seemed more like a faint call for help. I'd experienced something very similar—outside the same window—during a dream. Except in the dream, there'd also been a shadow lurking that had all but paralyzed me with fear as I wondered if someone was going to break in and hurt me. My wife heard my cries that night and thought I might be having a stroke. So when that call for help interrupted my email, that's where my mind went. I thought I might have misheard where the sound was coming from and she might be having a stroke in the next room. She wasn't, but it's strange how dreams and reality can sometimes parallel each other.

While I was still on the computer, I saw a post on our local neighborhood app about a little boy who'd just gone missing. As I was typing a comment that I thought I might've heard cries for help, a helicopter flew overhead, and multiple police cars parked on my street. I went outside to find neighbors across from my house searching for the boy. Which was a little odd. Because while he'd disappeared in my area, his house hadn't been anywhere close to mine. But wanting to help, I reported what I'd experienced and got involved.

I found out the little boy's name was Joseph. The fact that I'd been composing an email about Joseph of Arimathea when this Joseph got lost felt stronger than a coincidence. And I think it was. A lady responded to my comment on the neighborhood app later to let me know she'd found him by her house, which stood about three hundred yards from mine. It seemed unlikely that I would've heard his actual cries for help outside my window. But it did make me wonder if I'd heard him inside my head. As in God had let me hear the boy in a spiritual sense. If so, this wasn't one of my "ordinary" small-world phenomenon occurrences—this one came with a supernatural aspect.

The Importance of Focus

There could be times where God supernaturally gifts me with abilities beyond what I'm naturally capable of doing. I already told you I believe that happened when I played ping-pong at a championship level and when I prayed for and received instant healing of my elbow.

Most of the time, though, I think the Lord uses the gifts He's already given me—ones conducive to perceiving things like the small-world phenomena spiritual frequency. I once had a conversation about this with Marlene, one of the home health nurses, and what she told me made a lot of sense. She said the extreme focus required in her job didn't allow her the luxury to focus on "things unseen." I thought about that and realized that it was only after I'd started driving nurses around—a job that didn't require a

A God Thing

lot of concentration—that I began to more easily pick up on spiritual matters. My mind had the freedom and space to focus on those "things unseen." That job also afforded me the time to soak up spiritual knowledge and grow in my relationship with Jesus by listening to Christian talk radio. What a huge blessing.

Asperger's

One possibility for the kind of perception I have could be related to Asperger syndrome (AS). At the top of the autism spectrum, AS includes individuals who are typically high-functioning and have average or above intelligence. Oftentimes, people with AS are hard to spot. While I've never been formally diagnosed, books I've read on the subject make me think that if I did get tested, there's a high probability I'd fall into that diagnosis. Especially since the traits of AS can include gifts like seeing how numbers relate to other things and noticing patterns—two things I do every day. This ability has allowed me to discover the 409 Revelation and other small-world phenomenon spiritual frequency events.

On a sidenote, not all people who show this level of interest in numbers and patterns fall on the autism spectrum. It's just more common. But individuals not on the spectrum can be gifted this way too.

John S. Lee

My Family Tree

Another explanation could lie on the branches of my family tree. I've studied my family history back several centuries and traced my paternal line through my father Edward Norris Lee (1923-1980) to my grandfather Schely Lee (1900-1967), my great-grandfather Henry Albert Lee (1878-1949), and my great-great-grandfather Thomas Ruben Edwards (1849-1897). There's a chance through Thomas that I'm related to kings and queens of Scotland, England, and all over Europe. But the records are hard to follow. I did, however, discover that William Brewster (1566-1644), my eleventh great-grandfather, was an original signer of the Mayflower Compact and a key spiritual leader for the Pilgrims who landed on Plymouth Rock in 1620. I guess you never know who you might see on your family tree if you look back far enough.

Speaking of "seeing," I found out from my second cousin Bobbi—who shares ancestry with me to Thomas Ruben Edwards—that he was known as the town seer. Similar to a prophet, a seer has visions into the future through supernatural insight. He was called upon to do such things as helping people locate their lost family members. Thomas happened to be born in 1849. Here's what I see in those numbers. The first original date (1), the year (8), and the date (49) connects him to the 409 Revelation.

A God Thing

Also, his son Henry died in 1949, which reinforces the 409 Revelation.

Thomas's grandson—my grandfather Schely Lee—also had unique gifts. Gifts that seemed to skip a generation and my great-grandfather Henry. Schely had a special way with animals and a talent for dowsing, also called water witching. He could walk the land holding a forked stick and locate ground water, metals, and other objects. I witnessed my grandfather give a demonstration once. Ten people stood around him with their hands closed. One had metal hidden in his hand, and Schely found it. I guess there is something to that incredible talent.

As a descendant of those two men, could my gift have been genetically inherited? It's a distinct possibility. Especially if it did skip over a generation—my father—and jump down to me. Regardless, God can and does use any means which allows people to accomplish what He has called them to do.

Do you have any special gifts you feel God has given you? Or do you know of any special gifts within your family tree? Sometimes we might not notice them right away. But you could always pray and ask for Him to show you.

A Final Word

> *Trust in the Lord with all your heart,*
> *and lean not on your own understanding;*
> *In all your ways acknowledge Him,*
> *and He will direct your paths.*
> *Proverbs 3:5–6 NKJV*

God has a plan for everyone. He longs to have a relationship with you. Because of that, He offers each one of us opportunities to learn to listen for—and hear—His still small voice. If you're wondering how to tune into that voice, try starting with scripture. Get grounded in His Word. Read or listen to your Bible. Check out Christian radio programs and online sermons. Look into finding a church home or a Bible study if you don't already have fellowship with other Christians that way.

Most likely, the Lord will use what most interests you to get your attention. My small-world phenomenon discoveries, including the 409 Revelation, may not be universal to your world, but there is strong evidence that it applies to mine. I'm grateful that God works with the gifts He's given

A God Thing

me and made it possible for me to see so many interconnections in my life throughout the years. I've shown you my small-world phenomenon spiritual frequency, and I'm believing and praying that you will find yours.

Sources

If you're interested in any of the radio shows, pastors, or churches I've mentioned, here's some information:

- EndTime Ministries:
  https://www.endtime.com/
- The Prophecy Club:
  https://www.prophecyclub.com/
- *Faith, Hope, and Love*:
  https://www.calvarycathedral.org/sermon-series/radio-shows/
- *Renewing Your Mind*:
  https://renewingyourmind.org/
- Alex Jones at The Federal Reserve:
  https://youtu.be/IZ0EMSaVFpg
- Springcreek Church:
  https://www.springcreekchurch.org/
- Reunion Church:
  https://reunionchurch.org/
- North Cities Pentecostal Church:
  https://www.northcities.org/
- Turning Point Church (Jeff Wickwire):
  https://tpcfamily.org/people/wickwire/
- Tellingthetruth.org:
  https://www.tellingthetruth.org/

Notes

CHAPTER 1:
1. Pastor Keith Stewart. "Deliver Us from Me-Ville." Springcreek Church, Garland, Texas. Sermon. July 26, 2009.

CHAPTER 2:
1. Pastor Keith Stewart. "The Gift of Friendship." Springcreek Church, Garland, Texas. Sermon. July 8, 2012.
2. Mike Huckabee. FOX News. Interview with Laura Schoff, Author of *An Invisible Thread*. Jan. 5, 2013.

CHAPTER 4:
1. Dr. R.C. Sproul. *Renewing Your Mind*. Ligonier Ministries. 100.7 FM. Jan. 16, 2012.
2. Dr. R.C. Sproul. "Chance or Providence?" *Renewing Your Mind*. Ligonier Ministries. 91.7 FM. May 27, 2009.
3. Nancy Leigh DeMoss. *Revive Our Hearts*. 91.7 FM. May 28, 2009.
4. Irvin Baxter. *Politics and Religion*. EndTime Ministries. Oct. 15, 2009.
5. Pastor Keith Stewart. "Ghost, Part 1—Empowered." Springcreek Church, Garland, Texas. Sermon. June 2, 2019.
6. Irvin Baxter. *Politics and Religion*. EndTime Ministries. Jan. 6, 2010.
7. Irvin Baxter and Katherine Albrecht. *Politics and Religion*. EndTime Ministries. Nov. 10, 2009.
8. Pastor Bob Coy. *The Active Word*. Calverychapel.org. Jan. 7, 2010.

9   Pastor Keith Stewart. "A Reasonable Faith-Part 2: Science versus Scripture." Springcreek Church, Garland, Texas. Sermon. March 21, 2021.

CHAPTER 5

1   For more information about Father Suarez check out https://www.fernandosuarez.org/ and https://www.youtube.com/channel/UCkWJ3GAZLRT5fNOk8sIUKZQ
2   Pastor David Hood. "All You Leave Behind." Springcreek Church, Garland, Texas. Sermon. Dec. 27, 2009.
3   Pastor D.G. Hargrove. North Cities United Pentecostal Church, Garland, Texas. Sermon. Dec. 27, 2009.
4   Pete Briscoe. Tellingthetruth.org. April 16, 2010.
5   Pastor Keith Stewart. Springcreek Church, Garland, Texas. Sermon. July 4, 2021.
6   Irvin Baxter. *Politics and Religion.* EndTime Ministries. Sept. 1, 2010.

CHAPTER 7

1   Irvin Baxter. *Politics and Religion.* EndTime Ministries. Jan. 6, 2010.

CHAPTER 9

1   Alex Jones. *The Alex Jones Show*. Nov. 7, 2011.
2   409Revelation. "Alex Jones at the Federal Reserve." https://www.youtube.com/watch?v=IZ0EMSaVFpg&t=5s. Oct. 7, 2011.
3   U.S. Securities and Exchange Commission. Accessed August 20, 2013. https://www.sec.gov/Ar-

chives/edgar/data/45694/000115895708000380/f10k093008.htm
4. Wikipedia. Accessed August 20, 2013. https://en.wikipedia.org/wiki/Formula_409
5. Brianrouff.com. Accessed Jan. 31, 2014. https://brianrouff.com/when-myth-becomes-reality/

CHAPTER 10

1. Pastor Keith Stewart. Springcreek Church, Garland, Texas. Sermon. October 3, 2021.

www.ingramcontent.com/pod-product-compliance
Lightning Source LLC
Chambersburg PA
CBHW061657040426
42446CB00010B/1785